SUCCESS WITH
WATER-SA
GARDENS

SUCCESS WITH
WATER-SAVING
GARDENS

Graham Clarke

GUILD OF MASTER CRAFTSMAN
PUBLICATIONS LTD

First published 2007 by
Guild of Master Craftsman Publications Ltd
Castle Place, 166 High Street,
Lewes, East Sussex BN7 1XU

All of the pictures were taken by the author, except for those listed below:
Neville and Shirley-Anne Bell: front cover, Glenhirst Cactus Nursery.
GMC/Eric Sawford: pages 12, 125–127; 128 (right), 129–130, 132,
133 (right), 135–136, 137 (right), 138–141, 142 (left), 144, 145 (top),
146, 149 (bottom), 150, 151 (left), 153 (right); Hozelock: 38, 39 (top),
41 (top), 46, 63 (right); Lindum Turf: 94; Toro: 95 (top); Mr Fothergills'
Seeds: 119 (top right), 128 (left).

Illustrations by Penny Brown

ISBN: 978-1-86108-484-2

A catalogue record for this book is available from the British Library.

Managing Editor: Gerrie Purcell
Production Manager: Jim Bulley
Editor: Virginia Brehaut
Managing Art Editor: Gilda Pacitti
Designer: John Hawkins

Set in Futura

Colour origination by Altaimage
Printed and bound by Sino Publishing

Contents

LEFT This succulent *Agave americana* 'Variegata' is perhaps the epitome of a 'low-water' plant.

ABOVE **If you are permitted to use a hosepipe by law, make sure that it is used wisely – which generally means that you should completely soak an area rather than just wet it for a minute or two.**

Introduction

The subject on every gardener's lips at the moment is that of water, or rather the lack of it. Worldwide, we are being badly hit. Over the past few years most countries have had a dramatically reduced annual rainfall, which means that both the water tables and water reserves are low. And, on top of that, many places are enforcing watering bans (such as hosepipe bans), which exacerbates the problem as far as garden plants are concerned.

On a global scale the climate is changing. This can't be denied. But what is still very much debatable is the cause of this change. The overwhelming belief, although not 100 per cent conclusive, is that it is due to Man's interference with the flow and ebb of the world's various natural cycles. This is mainly caused by air and motor travel which have soared from practically nothing a hundred years ago, to today, when these things rank as the biggest man-made environmental threats the planet has ever seen. More recently huge construction projects are exacerbating the problem. These are taking place in various parts of the world, but if you think of the new cities to have been built over the past century and the increasing expansion of others, this is indeed a worldwide phenomenon.

In our domestic lives, we need to get on with our gardening and, being environmentally aware water-conscious gardeners, we have to do three things: i) use as little fresh water as we can get away with, ii) conserve as much rainwater as we can and iii) where possible, grow the types of plants that require less water.

It is my intention, with this book, to cover these three things as they relate to our various gardening preferences. For example, how can you save water when you are trying to establish a new lawn? How can you have lots of pots and containers in your garden when you know that they are thirsty and need watering more often than anything else? How possible is it to have a successful greenhouse, propagating and nurturing young plants, when water is at a premium? And which plants – specifically which annuals, biennials, perennials, climbers, trees, shrubs, fruits and vegetables, can survive in conditions with less water? All of the answers will be somewhere in this book.

AWARD OF GARDEN MERIT

Throughout this book you will see the initials AGM set after certain plants. This denotes that the plant in question has passed certain assessments carried out by experts under the auspices of the Royal Horticultural Society in Great Britain. Only plants with exceptionally good garden qualities can be awarded this special Award of Garden Merit.

LEFT Lawn grass is one area of the garden that does not need watering during a drought as in most cases the green grass will return after the first rains.

CHAPTER 1

The importance of water

ABOVE **Rainfall dampens the garden, but it also fills reservoirs and tops up the water table.**

T he title of this chapter could, more accurately perhaps, be 'Water is REALLY important!' For without it, neither you, nor I, nor any living thing on this earth would survive, including of course members of the plant kingdom. And because plants are the essential lifeblood of our own existence (all food derives from plants – even the animals we eat have fed off plants) we owe it to ourselves to understand how they 'work', and particularly the vital role that water plays in their well-being.

HOW DO GARDENS GET WATER?

When one says that a garden gets its water via rainfall, the statement is correct, yet does not tell the whole story. Yes, rainfall plays the major part in this, but there are other factors to account for than mere droplets of water falling onto plants from a great height.

To start with, there is every likelihood that it will not rain when you want it to, so if you are to nurture your plants you will need to supplement this natural rainfall with your own preferred form of irrigation (see Chapter 4). More often than not you will be irrigating your garden using water from a mains water supply, and this is supplied by your local water company, which stores the water in huge above- or below-ground reservoirs. An exception could be that you are permitted to extract water from a natural source – a river or well. It could be that you live remotely, where there is no mains water laid on (this was common a hundred years ago, but rarely occurs these days). Or possibly you have a business that needs to use a great deal of water, and you have been given a licence to extract water. This will be closely monitored, however, and you would be likely to have the permitted amount of water you can extract reduced during times of low supply, such as during a drought.

Plants in a garden also get their water from the water table. When it rains, the structure of the soil lets the water in, where it percolates between the grains and is drawn down by gravity. It eventually reaches the permanently saturated level known as the water table. This level may be a few inches beneath the soil surface, or a few feet, depending on where you are. The soil 'structure' also has a bearing on both the way the water table replenishes itself, and the general availability of water to plant roots as it meanders its way down from the surface (see Chapter 3). But, when it comes down to it, the aforementioned reservoirs, natural rivers, wells and of course the water table, are all topped up by rainfall.

HOW DO PLANTS USE WATER?

The taking up of water from the soil is an important function of plant roots, but only the finer fibrous roots are involved. Near the tips of such rootlets are the root hairs. These pass between the minute grains of which a soil is composed and come in close contact with the film of moisture that surrounds the soil grains.

Soil 'water' is normally a weak solution of various salts and this water is absorbed into the root via a process called 'osmosis': when two solutions are separated by a membrane through which water can pass, but which holds back the dissolved salts, then water moves into the stronger solution. This process will continue as long as the difference in solution strength is maintained. The cell sap in the root hairs is a stronger solution than that in the soil, hence water transfers into the plant.

From the root hairs the water passes from cell to cell, into the conducting channels of root and stem and then into the leaves. Most plants have a way of slowing down when water runs short. Their pores half-close as the cells that surround them become less distended. In a drought situation, they can close altogether, but as they do, growth slows and will eventually stop. It needs a water supply to complete the cycle, open the pores, and kick-start the plant back into life.

Did you know that 90 per cent or more of a soft, herbaceous plant may consist of water? It is this water, present within the plant, that keeps the soft young leaf and stem cells turgid, or plump and extended. But if water is in short supply this cell turgidity is lost so that the stems of herbaceous plants become limp, and the leaves droop and wilt. Should water shortage be prolonged, the plant will probably wither and eventually die.

ABOVE **90 per cent or more of soft, herbaceous plants (such as this *Eucomis autumnalis*) may consist of water.**

THE HYDROLOGICAL CYCLE

This is the rather grand term for something that every child is taught in class during their first few years at school, but which we rarely give thought to once we leave school. This is the name for the earth's water circulation system, that consists of evaporation, condensation, precipitation and flow. The last two factors are powered by gravity – whether they are tropical downpours or sea mists, mountain torrents, roadside ditches or city sewers, they are simply rainwater searching for its base level: the sea.

There is an old saying 'everything that goes up must come down'. The epitome of this is the hydrological cycle. Evaporation, fuelled by the sun's heat takes water up, and when it condenses in the atmosphere to form clouds, it gets too heavy and comes down as rain. Plants play a significant role in evaporation, in fact, second only to the sea. The process, called transpiration, the loss of water through a plant's leaves, amounts to the same thing as evaporation: passively presenting water to the atmosphere to be soaked up and vaporized by the sun's heat.

1 Most of the water that evaporates comes from the sea and other large bodies of water.
2 Transpiration (loss of water from a plant's leaves, such as this one from the tulip tree, *Liriodendron tulipifera*) is secondary.
3 The evaporation condenses in the cooler atmosphere to become clouds.
4 The water in the clouds gets too heavy and returns to earth as rain – as indicated here by a rainbow.
5 The water collects in rivers (such as the Thames, seen here) and flows in search of its base level, the sea.

HOW HAVE PLANTS ADAPTED TO THEIR ENVIRONMENT?

Just as plants vary in their requirements for light and temperature there are also wide differences in their water needs. And plant adaptations in relation to water supply are more pronounced. For example, those growing in or near water (such as waterlilies or bog plants) are called 'hydrophytes'. Most show rapid growth, frequent branching and overwintering by buds, tubers or rhizomes.

On the other hand, a large number of plant species, called 'xerophytes', have adapted their form and structure to cope with water shortage. This usually takes the form of a reduced leaf area, as with moorland heather and broom. Under extreme desert conditions plants, such as succulents and cacti, may survive without water for months or even years. Such plants have even dispensed with leaves altogether; their fleshy stems are not only very suitable for water shortage but also act as the leaves.

Intermediate between the hydrophytes and the xerophytes are the great majority of ordinary plants, called 'mesophytes'. These also show adaptations that reduce water loss. Thus many plants (such as the sage, or *Salvia officinalis*) produce a textured leaf, or others (such as lamb's ears, or *Stachys byzantina*) produce a mass of hairs on their leaves for this purpose. And various evergreens, such as laurel, have thick leaves with a waxy surface, which tends to restrict transpiration.

Unless plants receive adequate water their growth will be checked or prevented. But, conversely, too much water in the soil can be bad for plants as well, because the air in the soil is replaced by excess water, and the roots become waterlogged.

ABOVE Waterlilies (this is *Nymphaea* 'Perry's Pink') and other plants growing in or near to water, are called 'hydrophytes'.

ABOVE 'Xerophytes', such as heather, have evolved with a reduced leaf area, to cope with water shortages.

ABOVE Many plants (including *Salvia officinalis*, or sage; this is the purple-leaved form) have developed textured foliage in order to cope with conditions of reduced water.

ABOVE In desert conditions cacti and succulents, such as those in this display at a flower show, may survive without water for months — or even years.

ABOVE Lamb's ears (*Stachys byzantina*) has developed leaves with fine hairs — an example of another way that plants have evolved to reduce water loss during times of drought.

GLOBAL WARMING

A friend who always cornered me to ask about gardening matters once posed me a really tough question. He asked if global warming would mean a big change regarding what he might be be able to grow in his garden. He was clearly alluding to the fact that warmer temperatures across the globe generally are going to enable many temperate parts to grow tropical plants, and presumably therefore cold parts to grow temperate plants.

ABOVE Droughts — of which a typical symptom in the garden is cracked soil — are increasingly likely if global warming is a reality.

But unfortunately it's not as simple as that. Yes, average temperatures are increasing. You just have to look at news reports, and to see worrying footage of huge Arctic icebergs starting to thaw and break up, to realize this. However, we are talking about 'average' temperatures, not all temperatures.

For example, average winter temperatures are rising, and have been for the past 40 years. But there will always be some particularly cold snaps that surprise us after we have been lulled into believing that the winter is going to be mild. It means that any tropical plants you may dare to grow and keep outdoors over winter, would most likely die! It would be a brave gardener who, on the strength of the news reports, invested in some citrus trees, tender palms and a range of cacti, and planted them all outdoors in a cold climate, in the hope of growing them to maturity. It isn't going to happen – at least for a few more decades!

I believe that the more significant result of global warming, as far as gardeners are concerned, is the greater amount of cloud cover. This isn't something you hear much about. Of course, when the sun does shine, we are told not to sit out in it for more than a few minutes at a time. But then we have long periods when the numbers of sunshine hours are vastly down on the average.

In 2002, a report commissioned by the National Trust and the Royal Horticultural Society in the UK pointed to a future where green lawns become unsustainable. Dry summers, it said, will result in 'hosepipe bans' (correct so far), and lawn-less gardens, unless Mediterranean grass species like 'Saint Augustine' and 'Bermuda' are used. A year later, in October 2003, an Impacts of Climate Change on Horticulture symposium was held in America, prompted by the well-documented shift in the first-leaf and first-bloom dates of plants over the past several decades. Then in 2004,

the RHS Science Exchange, held in London, brought together leading scientists to discuss the future of gardening. The Society's head of science said that there was evidence to suggest there would be some frost-free winters during the next hundred years and that much of the landscape will be altered forever by climate change.

GLOBAL WARMING AND THE GARDENER

It's important stuff for all of us, but here's what I believe global warming means for the gardener:

1 Less rainfall overall, meaning that we should grow more drought-tolerant plants like silver-leaved herbs and succulents. And we should buy water butts (as many as we can comfortably fit into the garden). The aim of this book is to help you to cope with this particular aspect of my 'global warming scenario'.

2 More cloud cover, so we may find the ripening of some fruits (tomatoes, strawberries and apples) takes longer; we should aim to grow forms that take longer to ripen without rotting.

3 Higher average winter temperatures will enable us to grow a few more exotic plants outdoors, but we should also be prepared to invest in plant protection, such as horticultural fleece, just so that we have something to wrap around these tender plants when those really cold snaps are forecast! And, yes, we can perhaps think about growing a few more exotic looking plants that Victorian gardeners would have considered out of the question: the second half of this book includes a fair number of these.

19

CHAPTER 2

Design tips for the water-saving garden

It is all very well identifying that you wish to have a 'water-saving' garden, and the plant directory section of this book will tell you all about the plants you can grow in such a garden, but how do you ensure that it looks good? Starting with a blank piece of paper, can you create a water-saving garden that 'works' in design terms? It is not my intention with this book to design the perfect water-saving garden, as it could never be entirely relevant to the reader's needs and individual location. However, the following pages will be useful in highlighting the issues you will face when designing your own garden.

ABOVE **Some plants, such as these red hot pokers (*Kniphofia* 'Alcazar') enjoy a position in full sun — but adding shade to a garden can broaden the range of plants you can grow.**

SHADE CAN HELP

Statement: The driest gardens are the sunniest gardens. This is a fact of life. When the sun's energy (light and heat) falls upon a part of the planet, whether it is an open spot in your garden, or an area the size of the Sahara Desert, a significant amount of moisture from the surface of the ground will be lost through evaporation. Therefore, in order to reduce this moisture loss, it is a good idea where feasible to create some shade.

There are varying degrees of shade, and these can be effectively broken down into the following four categories:

1 Partial shade: This is an area of the garden that is shaded for part of the day, but also receives full sun at times as well. The area may, for example, be shaded by buildings in the morning, but is sunny for the rest of the day.

2 Dappled shade: The area in question here will have sunlight filtering through when the sun is in a certain direction. Many trees, particularly deciduous kinds that drop their leaves in the autumn, provide this form of shade. Their light foliage canopies allow through some of the sun's rays, but as the sun moves across the sky, so different areas are illuminated. Woodland plants are most suited to dappled shade.

3 Light shade: This is the shade cast by walls, buildings, hedges and so on, but with the area open to the sky. Therefore there may be little or no sun, but still the light is bright. The soil can also be dry in this situation, particularly immediately in front of a wall. Many garden plants can be grown here, such as ferns, forms of *Hosta* and even some climbing plants (including a few roses, which are normally regarded as sun-lovers).

4 Deep shade: This is where the light intensity is very low, and the area is quite dark and gloomy. Such conditions are found under large trees with dense foliage, particularly evergreens and conifers, as well as between large buildings, and basement gardens.

ABOVE **Light shade is the type of shade cast by walls, buildings, hedges and so on, but with the area open to the sky.**

ABOVE **Dappled shade, when sunlight filters through branches and foliage, is enjoyed by many types of woodland plant.**

It is the first two types of shade that can be created in a sunny garden in order to conserve soil moisture. Of course, the plants you choose to grow in these places will use up moisture themselves, but they are unlikely to use up as much as if the sun was beating down in the area all day every day. Plus, you are able to choose a wider range of plants to grow.

21

ABOVE **Trees and large shrubs help to provide shady areas — but do not let them get too big, and nor should you grow too many of them, otherwise the garden becomes unmanageable.**

CREATING SHADE

A combination of sunny and shaded areas gives a garden more character and as we have seen, shady spots will not dehydrate as quickly as sunny ones. So what can create shade in the garden? Here are the main options:

Large shrubs and trees: If you grow these anywhere in a garden they will help to provide shady areas, but the rule is not to overdo it. If you crowd too many into a space you will just create a dark garden. Deciduous trees with a light canopy of foliage provide the best type of shade – dappled – so if space permits try planting a few of these. A small grouping of them will develop into a mini woodland area, which will provide the right conditions for a host of garden plants you would not otherwise be able to grow. Remember, however, that trees can create dry spaces immediately under their canopies, so you should choose and site them carefully with this in mind.

ABOVE **Hedges can cast useful shade and act as boundaries and dividers in the garden.**

ABOVE **A free-standing pergola – this one is covered by** *Wisteria* **– can be placed anywhere in the garden.**

Screens and hedges: These are traditionally used as garden boundaries, but there is no reason why they cannot be used within the garden to divide areas – where space permits of course. Hedges can be either formal (with straight sides) or informal (comprising shrubs – often flowering types – but invariably with arching stems billowing into each other). Being a plantsman I would always recommend a hedge rather than a fence or brick wall, but sometimes the latter are more practicable. In this case you could create them from bricks or screen blocks; or you could use panel fencing or trelliswork. Any of these screens will have a shady side if they are suitably positioned, and this can be used to create a water-efficient part of the garden.

Hedges can comprise solid banks of green (as in conifer hedges such as yew or Leyland cypress), but informal hedges can be very colourful. Walls and fences need to have climbing plants grown up and over them in order to make them look appealing – unless, of course, you prefer the straight-lined, clinical, minimalist look.

Arches, pergolas and arbours: A simple archway may cast shade, but it may be too small to be meaningful. A pergola – essentially a series of two or more attached arches – is a different proposition, however, and when fully clothed with climbing plants would become a good shade provider. 'Arbour' is the name for a sitting area, originally to be surrounded by trees. Today it usually means a sitting area with a canopy of wood above you, very often designed simply to act as a shade from the sun. Up all of these structures you can grow a range of climbing plants to hide the sharp lines, and provide dappled shade.

A patio, or somewhere close to the house, is the best places for a pergola. This is so that one can entertain under it, and perhaps be sheltered from the heat of the summer sun. But a free-standing pergola can be placed anywhere in the garden. If it is away from the patio there needs to be a 'reason' for it in design terms. This could be, for example, to walk through it to see a little statue as a focal point, placed at the far end, or it can be designed as a walkway through to a vegetable or fruit-growing area.

Regardless of where and why you erect a pergola, the point here is that it provides useful shade. On a patio it could be set next to small raised beds where shade-loving plants can be grown. Alternatively, if your pergola is over a garden path you will need to grow plants in narrow borders on each side of the path. You should clothe the pergola with climbers (see the directory section pages 142–145).

Buildings: In addition to the main dwelling, which may or may not be casting useful amounts of shade, you could consider building other permanent structures. A summerhouse or gazebo, for example, usually has one or two solid sides; the remaining sides being fully open to sunlight. The shaded area immediately behind a summerhouse, if there is space, can be useful for planting. The same applies to garden sheds, garages and larger storage units. A greenhouse, although made of glass and seemingly transparent, does filter sunlight and on the darker side of it there will be useful dappled shade.

ABOVE Summerhouses provide respite from the sun for you, and they cast shade for certain shade-loving plants to enjoy.

XERISCAPING

At this point I should mention xeriscaping, which originated in the United States, and is a type of landscaping about which little is known in the rest of the world. It developed in the hot, dry south-western states, out of a need to save water. It makes use of items of hard landscaping such as rocks, cobbles, gravel, slate and even wood, to form an almost maintenance-free design.

The original aim of xeriscaping was to make the landscape appear as natural as possible, but more and more 'xeriscapers' are now starting to incorporate manufactured materials, such as brick and paving, into the schemes. But as far as plants are concerned, only drought-resistant plants are used, and are used sparingly, as points of focus. Whereas the designs are often considered 'uninteresting'

when compared with traditional forms of planting, it does have its benefits and can be quite attractive if well constructed.

For instance, the design may be such as to give an impression of movement. Small rocks or cobbles may be placed so as to symbolize a flowing stream, or bluish slate can be positioned to represent a large pond out of which larger rocks may protrude.

Slates placed on edge may represent water falling over a rock and a few pieces of white gravel can be used to suggest splashes. Other stone can also provide interesting variations in texture. As this style of gardening grows in popularity, I am sure we will see other kinds of materials, including brick, metal and ceramics incorporated into the designs.

ABOVE Sometimes a garden in the 'xeriscape' style can be designed to give an impression of movement – in this case bluish slate has been made to look like a flowing stream.

DESIGNING WATER STORAGE INTO THE GARDEN

As we have already identified, no living thing can exist without water, and when it comes to rainfall we need to capture it. There are tanks and water butts, there are sumps and buckets…

ABOVE **Rainwater tanks should be placed in a shaded area, otherwise the water can heat up and encourage the growth of bacteria and algae.**

but a garden that has a significant number of these spread around will be ugly. So, how should you design a garden with water storage in mind?

When plastic water butts became available, in the 1980s, there was a huge market, and gardeners were seen to be 'efficient'. Water butts were sold mainly as a convenience to gardeners who may have to walk some way to find an outside tap. The best market was for storing water in remote places, such as allotments, where mains water was rarely available. Then in the fashionable 1990s, modern and contemporary garden design did away with the utilities of such things as water butts (as well as compost heaps and washing lines… when sales of tumble driers in the home hit an all-time high).

However, water butts themselves have come back into fashion, this time in the 'politically correct' way: that of keeping them for the purpose for which they were designed – to store rainwater and therefore conserve our precious mains supply. Since the original water butt 'explosion', in the 1980s, it has become more common to have water meters installed, which means that there is also a financial incentive to use recycled water. More details on water butts, and how to use them efficiently, appear on pages 42–43.

In design terms, however, where should a water butt be placed? How can it be incorporated into the garden scheme without becoming an eyesore? Essentially, any large water container (a butt or an open tank), is best placed in a shaded area. It is not desirable for the water inside to be in the full glare of the sun as it will heat up – often to quite high temperatures. Natural rainfall that has been collected via roofs, gutters and downpipes will have attracted a number of impurities on its travels. High temperatures can materially alter the content and chemical balance, and bacteria in the water can quickly grow. This is when the water will turn green, and sometimes start to smell badly.

I have three water butts in my garden and all are situated in places where they are shaded for most of the day; although I find it is impossible to find a suitable permanently shaded place for them. Although I have a small wooded area that would be ideal, the idea of installing a butt here is flawed as there is no sensible way to collect the rainwater (which, in any case, would be deflected by the tree canopies). Therefore, the essence of siting water butts has to be to put them next to structures where there are gutters and preferably downpipes (otherwise you will need to install these as well). My three water butts are filled via water run-off from the house, the garage and the greenhouse. But you can place them anywhere else that provides a similar run-off: annexes, sheds, outhouses, conservatories, car porch and so on.

One company has now designed a water butt which is designed as a garden feature in its own right, with a wood-grain finish and barrel-type strapping to recreate the look of a hand-crafted, wooden water barrel of the past. The lid adds to the butt's attractiveness as it is designed to take the weight of a potted plant, so gardeners can immediately blend the butt into a surrounding planting scheme.

I suppose the ideal storage place for water, although not usually in a practical sense, is underground. Here it is out of the way, out of sight, and it does not use up valuable space in the smaller garden of today. However, the practical problems of structural installation, what to put over the top of it, and how to draw the water (some sort of pump would be required to push it up to garden level) make the concept impractical, unless you have the room and financial means to accommodate it.

ABOVE **Store water butts in an out-of-the-way place as they are not generally attractive to look at. However, they will need to be 'fed' water from the roofs of nearby sheds, greenhouses, conservatories or other buildings.**

IT'S IN THE SOIL

Finally, although not strictly included as part of the 'design' of a garden, it would be remiss of me not to mention the soil at this stage. As you will see in the next chapter, a garden created for the intelligent use of water MUST have a good soil, containing plenty of moisture-retaining humus. Whereas this is usually built up over months and years, there is actually no better time to start than when the garden is still a 'blank canvas'. It could be worth thinking about the wholesale purchase of well-rotted manure or compost, for incorporating into the majority of the growing areas of the garden, before too much is already planted.

CHAPTER 3

Good soils lead to good gardening

Creating a healthly soil is the key to creating a good water-saving garden. It's dirty. It's mucky. And if you're any sort of gardener, it gets right underneath your fingernails! The soil is without doubt the most important part of a garden, especially a water-saving one. It is the plants that make a garden beautiful, but none of them will grow without the soil, and the condition your soil is in can make the difference between a thirsty, water-guzzling plot and a beautiful, water-efficient garden.

ABOVE **Creating a balanced soil is the key to creating a garden that won't guzzle water.**

SOIL TESTING

Do you know how good or bad your soil is? If you live in a brand new house with just a bit of grass laid by the builder, chances are there won't be much topsoil (which may have been skimmed off and sold). The lawn could be laid directly on to muddy yellow sub-soil, and this could spell trouble for you and your garden over the years. It will take a lot of digging, conditioning and incorporation of manure or compost to bring it up to scratch. You might be better off buying in a load or two of good quality topsoil, into which you can immediately get planting!

But if you live in an older property, and the garden soil has been there a long time, with successive gardeners doing things with it (or not), just how can you tell if the soil is any good? And, just as important, how can you tell if it is the fabled 'acid' soil so loved by heathers, rhododendrons, camellias and *Pieris* or the 'alkaline' or chalky soil favoured by butterfly bushes and daphnes? Then there is the question of whether your soil is heavy with clay or light and sandy. And if you were into the subject in quite a major way you could also break it down to 'silt' and 'loam' soils. Oh yes, the soil is a very 'deep' subject!

ABOVE **A newly built house may have the garden 'laid to grass', or the soil may be completely bare. In either case you do not know how good the soil is, so you should test it.**

ABOVE *Azalea mollis* – a member of the *Rhododendron* family that needs an acid soil in which to thrive.

ABOVE *Buddleja* (this one is called 'Royal Red') is one of the plants that prefers a slightly alkaline soil.

BULKY ORGANIC MATTER

If you are growing vegetables, whichever soil you have you should dig it over once a year, and whenever possible incorporate plenty of well-rotted bulky organic matter – in other words compost or farmyard manure (if you can get hold of it). Manure is the best material if you want to feed the soil and increase its moisture-retaining capabilities; manure from pigs and horses is most commonly available, usually from farms that put up signs. Sometimes a town-based garden centre will be able to order it in for you. It is not particularly expensive but it is heavy and does not prevent weed growth – but it produces luxuriant plant growth. Poultry manure is also available to buy, but this is very strong and needs to dry out to use as a fertilizer dressing rather than manure.

Bulky manure is generally incorporated into the soil during digging. It improves the texture and fertility of the soil, and eventually decomposes into beneficial humus (complete decayed organic matter). The addition of such material is recommended for many soil types, including clay, where it helps to open up the

THUMB AND FINGER TEST

Across the globe there is a widely varying soil base. So, to tell you what kind of basic soil structure you have you could do the 'thumb and finger' test. Wet a sample of soil about the size of a ping-pong ball, and work it to break down all crumbs until it is smooth. Rub the sample between your thumb and fingers and assess it as follows:

1 If the soil feels soapy and silky, then it is a silt soil.
2 If it sticks slightly to the fingers and is slightly 'plastic', it is loam.
3 If it is very sticky and forms a glaze when rubbed, it is clay.
4 If it will not form a ball when rolled in the hand, then it is sand.

Before you plant anything you should have an idea of the soil's pH. This is the measurement of acidity/alkalinity in the soil, and you can test your own with a simple pH kit bought from the garden centre. You'll need to select samples of soil from various parts of the garden. The location of each sample should be recorded and each sample tested separately. The sample is placed in the tube supplied and a liquid added. The whole thing is shaken and then when settled you check its colour against a colour chart.

When you know the pH of the soil, you can choose all of the garden plants that are recommended in books for that level. If, however, there are other plants you want but they have the wrong pH requirements, then you can make the decision of whether to add lime to the soil (to make it more alkaline), or sequestered iron (to make the soil more acid). pH values start at 7.0; anything higher than this is alkaline, and anything lower is acid. The vast majority of plants like a slightly acid to neutral soil (that is, with a pH of 6.5–7.0).

You may think to yourself: why bother? Just plonk any plant in the garden and if it grows it grows, if it doesn't it dies! Well, while this may be true, it is an expensive way to go about your gardening. You see, a plant growing in the wrong soil may languish for years, with yellowing leaves, stunted growth, poor flowering and next to no fruiting. It will be a waste of time, effort and money!

ABOVE **If you are growing vegetables, whichever soil you have you should dig it over once a year.**

ABOVE **Animal manure (this is horse manure) should only be applied to the soil when it is well rotted.**

sticky soil, so improving the drainage of rainwater. Conversely, organic matter also helps free-draining soils such as sands, gravels and chalk, to hold on to moisture and plant foods, since it acts like a sponge.

The organic matter is added to the trenches while digging, at a rate of at least one level barrowload per 4sq yd (3.7m²). Digging should be carried out regularly on the vegetable plot and beds used for bedding plants, generally in autumn, and it should always be carried out prior to the planting of permanent plants (trees, shrubs, perennials and so on) and even before laying a lawn.

Apart from manure and homemade compost there are other forms of bulky organic matter. Peat (consisting of decomposed sphagnum moss or sedges extracted from bogs) is often recommended as a soil improver, but it has little

in the way of nutritional content and, more pertinent in this day and age, it is non-renewable. The 'farmed' bogs have taken thousands of years to develop, and then in a matter of days they are carved out and depleted. Purely as a soil conditioner, I would recommend other alternatives.

WHY WELL ROTTED?

Remember that the compost or manure has to be well rotted, otherwise if it rots while it is in the ground it can deplete the soil in the immediate vicinity of much needed nitrogen. It can also cause burning to plants if directly touching them.

ABOVE **Garden compost improves the texture and fertility of the soil.**

These include coconut fibre (coir fibre) from coconut husks. It is the short waste fibres and husk particles that are used for coconut matting, rope making and so on. It is very similar in appearance and texture to sphagnum moss peat, and retains moisture well. In fact, it was used in gardening 150 years ago but it never became really popular, presumably because peat was accepted as the better soil conditioner.

Bark (pulverized or shredded) can be added to the soil during digging. It should, however, be partially composted (or decomposed) and it should state this clearly on the bag. The benefit of this is that when it degrades further in the soil it will not deplete the soil of nitrogen. Bark is especially good at improving the drainage of, and opening up, heavy clay soils.

OTHER SOIL IMPROVERS

If you have a clay soil, you will know that after winter rains it becomes a sticky quagmire, and in the heat of the summer it bakes hard like concrete. Neither condition is appropriate to good plant growth, so you should do something about it. Certainly adding one of the bulky organic matters discussed previously will do wonders, particularly over a period of time. However, there are three 'inorganic' types of improver that, in their own way, are just as important, depending on the pH level of your soil. Therefore, before applying these you should conduct a soil test so that you can decide whether you want to apply them.

Lime: This is useful for adding to sticky clay soils. It improves the soil texture and makes it easier to cultivate. Sprinkle lime on to dug ground during autumn and allow it to lie over winter, then fork it in. If manure has been applied during the digging, wait a few months before applying lime, as it can react badly with the manure. Testing the soil in advance of application is particularly important in the case of lime, as lime increases the alkalinity of a soil. Do not apply lime if you have a lime-free (acid) soil and want it to remain acid for growing lime-hating plants, such as heathers, rhododendrons and camellias. For an excessively acid soil, below a pH5 level, some lime is recommended. If your soil is already quite alkaline, say pH8, then do not use more lime, as you will be creating an excess of it and there will be few plants that can tolerate this high level. A pH of 6.5 to 7.0 is ideal for most garden plants and vegetables.

Applying lime to a clay soil should be done once in every five years, but a sandy soil is different. In this case every two or three years will be sufficient, as the lime will be washed out by rain. If needed, use ground limestone or hydrated lime. The amount you apply will be based on the soil test, and there should be a guide supplied with the testing kit. An alternative to lime, but with a similar effect, is the use of calcified seaweed. This is like a type of coral, comes in packs from the garden centre and contains a number of minor plant foods. It is relatively expensive, however.

Gypsum: This is sulphate of lime, and is used on clay soils to improve texture and workability, and to reduce stickiness. Unlike lime, however, gypsum does not increase alkalinity in the soil so can safely be used on soils with a high pH level. It is also ideal for acid soils if you do not want to raise the pH. It should be applied in the autumn after digging, as for lime. Apply at the rate of 8oz per sq yd (226g per m²).

Coarse sand or grit: If you dig in a 2in (5cm) deep layer 8in (20cm) below the surface of a clay soil, it will have the effect of opening it up and allowing rainwater to drain through more easily. Both are obtainable in bulk from builders' merchants and in smaller bags from garden centres.

ABOVE **Coarse sand, along with grit, is available from builders' merchants, and can be used to break up a clay soil.**

ABOVE **Adding lime to a clay soil improves the soil texture and makes it easier to cultivate — but check the pH of the soil beforehand, or you could make it too alkaline for the plant you want to grow.**

ABOVE **Peelings and unused bits of vegetables – and old tea bags – can be added to the compost heap.**

ABOVE **If you are adding woody items, such as conifer and hedge clippings, to the compost heap, make sure they are shredded into small pieces.**

MAKING COMPOST

One thing I am very keen to promote with all gardeners is the art of recycling garden waste. Of course, another word for this is composting. Here is the biology lesson: all living things eventually die, and in the case of plants it tends to be quite often. Annuals come to the end of their lives every autumn; biennials at the end of their second year; perennials after a number of years when they've become too old or we've become fed up with them and dug them up. And then, of course, there are weeds: these tend to die whenever I can get hold of them! All of these things can be put on to a compost heap. They'll rot down to a fraction of their former size, and in so doing will become good, available humus off which other plants can grow.

Other things to add to a compost heap include peelings and unused bits of vegetables from the kitchen, as well as grass mowings, shredded prunings and any other bits of soft, green matter. Even small amounts of paper, if shredded by an office shredder, can be added. I mention the fact that the prunings need to be shredded: trees and shrubs that have been pruned are, by definition, very woody, and wood tends to take forever to rot. However, the smaller the woody bits the quicker they'll rot. In essence, soft things are best for a compost heap, so the rule is: the harder the material, the smaller it should be.

In an ideal world you want the contents of the heap to rot in the quickest way, so that you can make use of the resulting crumbly compost. So, do not put too much wood in or onto it, even if the wood is shredded. In fact, do not put too much of anything on to a compost heap, as the secret to making good compost is the 'little-and-often' principle. You should aim for a really good mixture of things.

What should NOT go on to a compost heap? Well, aside from general household rubbish of plastics, metals and glass, more or less anything else can. It is not advisable, however, to add cooked food – meat, fish, cheese and grease. Aside from smelling bad (rotting meat and dairy food smells completely different to rotting raw vegetable matter), you could be encouraging rats and other unwanted visitors. Also, don't add the roots of perennial weeds such as couch grass, ground elder, bindweed, docks and dandelions. These will almost certainly continue to grow and you'll end up spreading them around the garden.

What about the structure of the heap? Take a trip to the garden centre and you'll discover a range of enclosed bins to keep the area nice and neat and tidy. If you are a little less fastidious about things at the 'working' end of the garden, you could simply knock together four upright posts and encircle them with chicken wire. The edges will become dry and will take longer to rot, but inside the heap things should rot down nicely.

Making good compost can take as little as six weeks, if it is the height of summer and you add just small bits of green matter and some activator – usually a nitrogen-based substance that speeds up the rotting process. Or it can take a year or more, if there are lots of thick, dry autumn leaves, or a fair amount of shredded wood, or you started the heap in the autumn (the speed of rotting decreases in winter).

The end result of all your hard work will be a wonderful, friable, dark, fine material that can be dug into the soil, used as a mulch or even, if it is fine enough, used as a seed compost. This, to me, is recycling in the best sense! You can create your own leafmould by laying down rotted leaves, collected and compressed over several years. It adds fibre to the soil, improves drainage and helps to retain moisture. You can rarely find this to buy, however, which means making your own the practical option – but only if you have access to many broad-leaved trees!

ABOVE **Making good home-grown compost can take as long as a year, or as little as six weeks (in the summer).**

WHAT TO PUT IN YOUR COMPOST HEAP

Do put on the heap:
◆ annual weeds
◆ vegetable scraps and peelings
◆ grass mowings and soft green matter
◆ shredded prunings
◆ shredded paper

Do not put on the heap:
◆ perennial weeds
◆ plastics, metals or glass
◆ cooked food – especially meat, fish or cheese

MULCHING

This is a key factor in any garden that is designed to use water sparingly. Essentially, a mulch is a layer of organic (or inorganic) material applied around plants and on top of the soil surface. Putting down a mulch is our way of copying the natural state of meadows and pastures with their accumulation of dead herbs and grasses on the soil surface; in a shady garden mulching effectively recreates the forest floor with its fallen leaves. There are several benefits in putting down a 2in (5cm) layer of mulch spread over a warmed, moist soil in spring. Preventing evaporation is the first. Suppressing weed growth is another (if they do seed in the mulch they are easily pulled up). And a third benefit is that the mulch will gradually add to the soil humus content of the soil through the action of earthworms.

What are the materials to use for mulching? Homemade composts and leafmould are full of plant goodness and are certainly the easiest of products to get hold of – or make yourself. Farmyard manure is also excellent, but a ready supply is not so easily sourced. Again, these materials should be applied when they are well rotted. If applied in a raw state, their composite strength (acidic and high in ammonia) could damage the soil or any live plant material it touches. In fact, even in its well-rotted state, it should not be laid so that it touches the plants, as it will cause 'burning'.

Bark is fairly cheap, light and biodegradable and has excellent moisture-retaining and weed-suppressing qualities. It is available in colours other than 'natural'. In commercial landscaping, bark in green, gold and black chips is highly

ABOVE **Putting down organic mulch, here around roses, suppresses weeds, helps retain soil moisture and aids soil nutrition.**

ABOVE **Cocoa shell mulch is becoming increasingly popular – and it can even make the border smell of chocolate for a week or two!**

ABOVE **Fabric mulches, although not particularly good to look at, do prevent weed growth and reduce soil evaporation.**

popular, but for domestic gardens the tendency is usually to go for something more natural in colour. The disadvantage to using bark is that it needs topping up most years, and its appearance is not always to everyone's taste. It is, however, an excellent surface for pathways, and is safe where children are running about.

Cocoa bean shells, coir fibre and even hair mulches are available. There are also a number of different fabric mulches for allowing rain through, but preventing (or at least reducing) water evaporation from the soil. Many alpines and rock plants are happiest when a layer of stone chippings or small-grade gravel is laid around them. It stops water and mud splashing up on to the leaves. Stone mulches are long lasting and there is a huge range of colours and size grades to choose from. The disadvantages to using them, however, are worth noting. To start with, in the autumn when leaves fall it is difficult to sweep or clear the area. A thin layer of gravel will afford some moisture retention in the soil, but

to do this effectively the layer should be thick – 3in (7.5cm) or more. No matter how thick a gravel mulch, weeds will always seem to germinate in it, but fortunately they are usually quite easy to remove. It is advisable, but not essential, to lay down a weed-preventing membrane (widely available from garden centres) before putting down the chips. A very popular alternative to natural yellowish or brown gravel is chipped slate, in attractive, muted shades of blue, grey or plum.

Finally, glass nuggets are being used more these days as a decorative mulching material. This may sound dangerous, but it is safe to be around as the sharp edges have been rounded off during the manufacturing process. It has very similar qualities to gravel, but is much more expensive and does not always blend well with the planting schemes in traditional gardens. It is available in a range of bright colours; modern garden designers often use it as part of their more contemporary schemes.

CHAPTER 4

Watering plants wisely

With the concern over future water shortages, and the consequent bans on garden watering which seem to occur more frequently these days, it is important not to waste water. Home water metering and therefore water on a pay-per-use basis, plus the fact that the cost of having water supplied is continually rising, are both good reasons for conserving water at home. We have seen how important it is to have water butts and tanks, and also how to integrate them into the garden to reduce their aesthetic impact. But what about using the water in the most efficient way? How is it best applied and, more importantly, how should we use it without wasting it?

ABOVE **With concern over future water shortages, it is important not to waste water.**

WATERING EQUIPMENT

There are several items of irrigation equipment that any good gardener should have, let alone the water-wise gardener:

WATERING CAN

This is one of the first items of kit any new gardener should acquire, and it provides the most direct and efficient watering of any device. Watering can sizes vary, from a house plant can holding about 2½ pints (1.5 litres) of water to a mighty 2 gallon (10 litre) can. The larger the can, the stronger you will need to be to carry it around. Whichever design and colour of modern plastic watering can you opt for boils down to simply a matter of personal preference. It is a shame that shops selling these items do not have a 'sample' can filled with water for you to lift, hold, carry and pour, because it is one of the types of product you need to get a 'feel for'.

The old-style metal watering cans are coming back into fashion. They usually have relatively long spouts (which makes for easy point and direction of water flow); they do take some beating. The only other point I should mention about watering cans is the 'rose'. This is the 'cap'

to attach to the end of the spout; in it are dozens of small holes. The water flowing through these holes comes out as a fine spray, and is perfect for young, small or delicate plants (such as seedlings) to prevent them from being washed away by the force of a powerful spurt of water. Make sure the rose fits the spout firmly – if it is loose it will either fall off (which could be disastrous) or it can dribble badly which can be very irritating, and ruin a nice, level compost. If you wish for a wide area to be covered with the watering can, turn the rose so that the holes face upwards; this shoots the water over a large distance.

ABOVE **The sizes of watering can vary, so remember not to buy one that will be too heavy, when filled, for you to carry.**

ABOVE **A watering can fitted with a 'rose' means that you are able to water tender plants and seedlings without disturbing them or washing away the soil.**

HOSEPIPES

Hosepipes vary in aperture size, length, strength, durability, material from which they are made and, of course, in price. Essentially, however, you get what you pay for. The cheaper kinds, regardless of the length, will not last you as long as the thicker, reinforced pipes. The reason why you will often see a criss-cross of strengthening wires set within the clear plastic of a pipe is to avoid, or at least reduce, kinking. A thin pipe, especially if it is a few years old and has degraded through prolonged exposure to the elements, can kink so much as you haul it around the garden, that you can be infuriated by it. If you have a long garden, you may not easily find a hosepipe that extends all the way to the bottom. In this case you can buy a second hose and attach the two ends together with a suitable connector.

Storage of hosepipes can become an issue as well. They are very unsightly if left trailing across the garden when they are not in use. These days it is convention to purchase a reel, around which the hosepipe should be coiled when it is not being used. The better reels are those attached to the outside wall of the house, in close proximity to the outside tap, to which the hose is permanently connected. If you do not want to make the hose reel a 'fixture' you can buy a free-standing reel; this can be stored anywhere that is convenient. It is best to keep hosepipes out of the main glare of the sun (which will weaken the plastic and reduce the pipe's useful 'life'). Equally, in winter the pipe is best stored in a dry, frost-free shed. If any water remaining in the pipe freezes it could cause cracking – another reason to buy the stronger, reinforced types.

SPRINKLERS

As you will see below, sprinklers can waste water. However, if they are right for you they can be very effective at delivering water to where it is needed. There are three basic designs available: the rotary sprinkler, the oscillating sprinkler and the sprinkler hose.

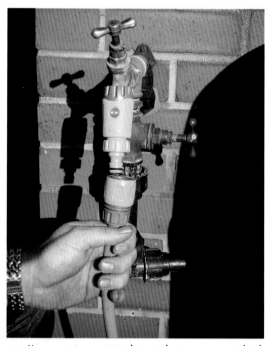

ABOVE **Many countries now insist that outside taps are connected with a non-return valve. This is where a valve is incorporated into the connector which prevents a backflow of contaminated water, such as from a pond or a sprayer containing chemicals, back into the mains water system.**

ABOVE A simple garden sprinkler such as this throws out a spray of water in a circular pattern.

Rotary sprinklers throw water over a circular area up to 25ft (7.5m) across. Some models can be set to spray only part of a circle. Oscillating sprinklers throw water over a square or rectangular area, which makes it easier to get water into a corner of the garden without drenching your neighbour! A sprinkler hose – a tube with tiny holes along one side – will water a narrow strip. With the tap turned low, this type can be converted into a drip irrigation system for a single row of plants.

DRIP IRRIGATION SYSTEMS

It is also possible to purchase, at reasonable cost, a complete drip-irrigation system for the whole garden (or a section of it, or perhaps just for use in the greenhouse). Pipes and branches of pipes with pre-drilled holes along their length can be laid throughout the area to be watered. They can even be sited strategically to get close to specific plants – or, more accurately, the root area of specific plants. When they are connected to a tap and it is turned on, the water seeps out of the holes and soaks the immediate area.

This type of system is very efficient in its use of water, but it can lead to a high percentage of evaporation if the water drips on to soil in full sun, especially if the soil is compacted and the water is not absorbed readily. However, you can negate this by activating the system to come on at night by using a timer device.

TIMER DEVICES

If one is employing a sprinkler or drip irrigation system, control is essential if water is not to be wasted. Whether the drip system is fitted to the mains water supply or to a rainwater storage tank, it is all too easy to leave the tap on by accident, with the subsequent waste of water. It is useful, therefore to purchase a timer-controlled water valve, which enables a regular watering scheme to be established. Again, this must be monitored as watering requirements will vary with the seasons and weather conditions.

ABOVE **Drip irrigation hoses such as this one are very efficient at directing water to the places where it is needed, with minimum evaporation and very little wastage.**

ABOVE **Using a timer device connected to an outside tap, and to your watering system, means that the garden can be watered even when you are absent.**

41

COLLECTING RAINWATER FOR STORAGE

If a water butt is fitted with a lid to exclude the light, the condition of the water will remain good for long periods. Most purpose-made butts come already fitted with a tap, which makes filling a watering can or bucket an easy job. The static pressure from a butt placed directly on the ground is fairly low – and it will be practically impossible to get a watering can underneath the tap. Therefore you should raise the butt off the ground, and sit it on piers of bricks, blocks or old paving slabs.

RIGHT **If a water butt is fitted with a lid to exclude the light, the condition of the water will remain good for long periods.**

BELOW **If your demand on water is great, or you simply want to harness as much rainwater as possible, you can link several water butts together so that when one fills it overflows into another. The number of butts you can link in this way is only determined by the amount of space available.**

Large water tanks and even large water butts should be permanently connected to the gutters and downpipes of the house. However, there are devices available from DIY stores that can be inserted in the down pipe (generally 68mm round or 65mm square pipes) in order to divert water in to the butt or tank.

USING 'GREY' WATER

In times of drought it is not unusual to find gardeners using bath or shower water on their plants because, once cool, it is perfect for use in the garden. It is possible to store such domestic water when rainwater is no longer available. By fitting a diverting valve on the bath or shower outlet so that it can supply the garden water storage system, it is possible to supply cooled bath water direct to the roots of plants – at any time of year.

Ordinary household soaps – which are used in such small quantities and then heavily diluted – will not harm plants. If you are concerned, however, it is not a difficult operation to install a simple replaceable, or washable filter. The types of water that should not be used on the garden include toilet waste, the waste from washing machines and dishwashers (as some detergents contain chemicals that are harmful to plants), and also the water from when cleaning a bath if a chemical cleaner was used.

ABOVE **If you have a large garden, or an allotment, and there is no mains water supply nearby, you will need to store as much water as you can to make life more easy.**

ABOVE **Washing up water is good for re-using in the garden during a drought, as long as you use ordinary washing-up liquid, and not bleach or other strong chemicals for cleaning.**

HOW IS WATER WASTED?

The most wasteful way of irrigating plants is the indiscriminate use of overall watering, such as using one of the sprinkler types mentioned earlier. Often the sprinklers are placed so that much of the water falls on to paving and patios where it simply runs away. Or sprinklers are put into a position where they water plants that do not require it. However, sprinklers are the sensible option for any closely planted areas, such as borders of perennials in full leaf and/or flower, or beds of thickly planted summer bedding which, in both cases, means that you may not be able to see the soil between the plants. Sprinklers can also be beneficial if it is your desire to use a foliage spray of water to clean plant leaves of harmful dust and dirt, especially if your garden is adjacent to a main road. In this instance, just make sure that you are not going to be inadvertently spraying water on passers-by!

ABOVE **Do not splash water indiscriminately on to foliage or hard surfaces, where it will do no good.**

Another common way in which water is wasted is when the gardener, who perhaps is a beginner or not knowledgeable about such things, splashes water around, often on to foliage where it can remain or easily evaporate, or on to hard surfaces where it runs off. With this type of gardener, if the soil is made darker by having water splashed on to it, they feel that the area has been sufficiently watered, and they move on. In truth, this is the worst kind of watering, for not only is it wasteful of water, but it can actually cause harm to the plants. When there is just a small amount of surface water, plant roots can detect it and they grow towards it, which means that they travel towards the surface. This is fine if the soil receives regular watering or is permanently moist, but can be fatal if the soil is not watered again and the soil bakes dry in an unforgiving sun. An indication of appropriate water quantities is provided below.

A third way in which water is wasted is that of timing. If you water plants during the heat of the day, then very often the water on the soil surface, and the surfaces of many leaves, flowers and stems, will quickly evaporate, and do no good at all. In fact, water droplets on some thin-tissued plants can act as a magnifying glass when the sun is strong, and this can cause burning to the plant – a condition known as scorching. It is much better to apply water in the evening when there is little evaporation. Early morning, before the sun rises too high in the sky is another preferred time, but is not as efficient.

ABOVE **Do not water plants during the heat of the day as much of the water will evaporate before it can do any good.**

WATERING GARDEN PLANTS

Established plants growing in soil in the garden are generally at less risk of drying out. The soil around them, being in such mass, usually has some moisture in it for them to use (plants in containers, however, are a different proposition; see below). You should really only start watering garden plants when the top 1in (2.5cm) or more of soil in beds and borders has become dry. And then, rather than water everything in sight, you

ABOVE **Plants most at risk of drying out are newly planted trees, shrubs, conifers, climbers and roses — which are all vulnerable for up to two years after planting; check them for dryness regularly and when you do water them, do it thoroughly.**

should decide which plants take priority. In other words, which are most at risk from drying out?

Plants most at risk include newly planted trees, shrubs, fruits, conifers, climbers and roses, which are all vulnerable for up to two years after planting. Newly planted perennials are at risk for up to a year after planting. Bulbs do not generally need too much watering after planting, as they have certain reserves of moisture within the bulb structure. Summer bedding plants must be watered regularly for the first month after planting after which they are generally able to tolerate drier conditions.

Another group of plants that take priority when it comes to watering are the vegetables. There are some types that are described as particularly 'thirsty', and these include celery, lettuces, early potatoes, runner beans, spinach and tomatoes. It may be wise to avoid growing these types if your area is prone to low rainfall and hosepipe bans.

Except for conifers, which benefit from watering through their foliage, most plants take up water through their roots (as we saw in Chapter 1). To be truly efficient, a watering system should supply water to root level whilst keeping evaporation and seepage to a minimum. An excellent way to water trees and shrubs involves an extra process at planting time. Sink vertical sections of earthenware drainpipe into the ground so that one end of the pipe is slightly above the plant roots – and even proud of the soil (but not too proud, or it will become obtrusive). The pipe should then be filled with very coarse gravel. It is then both easy and efficient to direct water into the pipe, using a watering can.

There is also the question of how much water to apply. You should certainly supply enough water to moisten the soil to a depth of at least 6in (15cm). To achieve this you will need to apply the equivalent of 1in (2.5cm) of rain. This equates to roughly 5 gallons of water per square yard (27 litres per m²). When watering with a sprinkler you can measure the amount being applied by standing some tins or jam jars within the area being watered. When they contain 1 in (2.5cm) of water you know you have supplied enough. Purpose-made rain gauges are available from some garden centres and hardware stores, and these will give you the same information.

It cannot be disputed that the most economical way to water plants is to do it individually. This is certainly feasible with larger plants such as trees, shrubs, climbers, conifers and so on. With 'specimen' plants like these you could 'basin-plant' them – which obviously needs to be done at planting time, not when they are established in the ground. This method

of growing is when the plant is set in a shallow depression. It will help to stop water from running away, and is particularly effective at catching rainwater.

The amount of water to apply to specimen plants will depend on their size and, to some extent, on the species. An approximate guide would be 1 gallon (4.5 litres) of water for each smaller plant, up to 4 gallons (18 litres) for larger plants. Apply the water slowly so that there is no overflow or run-off.

In terms of watering specific areas of the garden, such as plants in containers, as well as trees, shrubs and border plants, and greenhouses, frames, cloches, conservatories, lawns and the kitchen garden, Chapters 5 to 9 will provide detail.

WATER QUANTITIES: FACTS AND FIGURES

Those who have water meters fitted to their mains water supply have probably found ways of making savings. Even stopping what appears to be a minor waste, such as curing a dripping tap, or not having water running when brushing your teeth, very quickly adds up to considerable savings over a year. Other savings can be made in and around the home. For instance, the average bath uses approximately 30 gallons (135 litres) of water, whilst a five-minute shower only uses around 14 gallons (65 litres); a saving of 16 gallons (70 litres) could be made every time one showers instead of bathing. The water-collecting potential of a three- or four-bedroom house is considerable. For example, with an average rainfall, the roof of a house may collect as much as 11,000 gallons (50,000 litres) of rainwater per year.

ABOVE **Saving water is the duty of all of us. When using outside taps make sure you turn them off afterwards – and if the tap drips, get it fixed.**

CHAPTER 5

Container gardening

One of the easiest ways to add colour and interest to a garden – without the need for heavy garden construction or reconstruction, or complex soil preparation – is to use containers: troughs, pots, tubs, urns, vases, hanging baskets, windowboxes and even growing bags. The first five can be positioned on any hard surface, but if you site them in a shady spot you must ensure that shade-loving plants are chosen. Hanging baskets and windowboxes, by definition, should be attached to buildings or vertical walls, and both types can raise the colour level – literally.

ABOVE Container plants need not just consist of vibrant summer flowers – foliage shrubs, such as the golden-leaved Mexican orange blossom (*Choisya ternata* 'Sundance' AGM) can make stunning displays.

WHAT ARE JOHN INNES COMPOSTS?

The range of John Innes (or JI) composts are frequently quoted, but few gardeners truly understand the differences between them. They are actually soil-based composts made to formulas devised through research at the John Innes Horticultural Institute in Norwich, England. There is a seed compost used for raising seedlings, and sometimes to root cuttings, plus three potting composts.

You can easily buy all of these composts from good garden centres, bagged and clearly indicating which is which. Or you can make up your own, using the ingredients listed below (but you would need to purchase sterilized loam, or sterilize your own loam at home – which is not something the average gardener would wish to do). The various composts comprise the following ingredients (all parts by weight).

Seed compost: 2 parts sterilized loam, 1 part fibrous peat, and 1 part coarse sand. To each bushel (2220 cubic in/36,000 cubic cm) there is 1½oz (43g) superphosphate of lime and ¾oz (21g) of ground chalk.

Potting compost No 1 (for seedlings to move into from the seed compost): 7 parts sterilized loam, 3 parts fibrous peat, and 2 parts coarse sand. To each bushel (2220cubic in/36,000 cubic cm) add ¾oz (21g) of ground chalk plus 4oz (113g) of a chemical mixture made up of 2 parts hoof and horn meal, 2 parts superphosphate of lime, 1 part sulphate of potash.

Potting compost No 2 (for potting on young plants): same mixture but double the quantity of fertilizers.

Potting compost No 3 (for raising plants to maturity): same mixture as No 1, but treble the quantity of fertilizers.

ABOVE **There are so many different types of bagged compost for sale, it pays to know what your plants need, so you can buy them the most appropriate sort.**

POTS, TUBS, URNS AND VASES

There is a wide range of these types of container available, made from wood, plastic, terracotta, reconstituted stone and moulded resin. The plastic ones are the cheapest but some are rather garish so look for those that are not too obtrusive. The most popular colours for plastic are white, green and brown. These containers are best used for seasonal displays of annuals (mainly bedding plants) and bulbs. When in full flowering glory, they make very effective focal points. They are, of course, ideal for standing on a patio, path, driveway, or next to a door. But they can also look very good when stood in borders. The tubs, raised on blocks, can be placed in a part of the garden that is not at its best when the plants in the tub are prettiest.

Permanent plants, such as small trees (dwarf fruit trees can be very successful), conifers, flowering shrubs and even some perennials (such as forms of *Hosta*) can look fabulous in containers – although they do not necessarily have the long summer of vibrant colour that you can get with annuals. If you live on a chalky soil you will find that it is not possible to grow successfully most of the plants and shrubs from the heather and *Rhododendron* family (including *Azalea*, *Camellia*, *Pieris* and many others). These are 'ericaceous' plants, meaning that they need an acid soil. The beauty of growing these permanent plants in a large tub is that you can supply them with one of the ericaceous composts widely available from garden centres, and they will they grow happily in your chalky garden.

PLANTING A TUB

1 Start by adding drainage material, such as gravel or broken crocks, into the bottom of the tub; about 2in (5cm) thick. Do not completely block the drainage holes in the bottom of the pot (if there are no drainage holes, then you should drill some).

2 Add the compost of your choosing; the more 'open' the compost (such as peat or coir), the quicker it will dry in sunny weather. Fill about two thirds of the tub firming down as you go. Mix water-retaining granules into the compost as you plant. Some composts now include granules as standard.

ABOVE **Box (*Buxus sempervirens*) makes an excellent container plant — it is evergreen, and is slow growing.**

ABOVE **Modern and contemporary containers can be attractive in their own right; complex-looking containers are best seen with simple plants that are plain in leaf or form.**

3 Set the plants in the tub where they are to go. As a guide, one plant in the centre and four or five around the edge of the tub 12in (30cm) across is about right. Set each plant so that the surface of its root ball is 1in (2.5cm) below the rim of the tub.

4 Fill around the rootball with more compost; adding smaller plants as you go, eventually filling in all around them. You can add water-retention granules at this stage, too

5 Firm all of the plants in place and then water them in. Water regularly throughout the lives of all container plants. Placing a tray underneath will make a water reservoir.

HANGING BASKETS

Even if you live in a flat you will have room for a hanging basket outside a window or on a balcony, so there is no excuse! Every garden centre and plant market sells ready-planted hanging baskets. If time is short and your pocket is deep, by all means invest in one of these. But do go for sturdy baskets, nicely planted with quality plants. Often you will find very cheap and shabby baskets at supermarkets; you will probably be very disappointed with these. But if you buy all the ingredients and plant up your own basket(s) you will have control, not only over what plants go in, but also over the quality and content of the compost you use.

There are a number of different basket types available. The wire basket is the traditional type; the soil within it is kept in place using a basket liner. Sphagnum moss was the old traditional material for lining baskets as it was lightweight, looked natural and was readily available. Although you can still find this occasionally, it is somewhat frowned upon these days as harvesting sphagnum depletes a natural habitat of it, harming the indigenous wildlife.

These days man-made fabric liners in green, brown or black do the job just as well. If you do use moss, make sure you line the basket with polythene as well; otherwise, if birds steal the moss, all the compost will fall out.

There are also plastic baskets available, with filled-in sides, and in many ways these are easier to manage. To start with they dry out less quickly, and some types have a built-in water reservoir or tray to make the chore of watering less frequent. Make sure that the plastic basket you choose has holes in the side in order for trailing plants to be positioned – these will help to create an attractive basket much more quickly.

Traditionally, baskets would be home to plants of different shapes and sizes, but these days simplicity is often called for. I have grown baskets with just one plant – the magnificent *Petunia* Surfinia – and as long as it is well fed and watered, and placed in a sunny spot, this can fill the basket with flowers of a single, dramatic colour. Do not forget to place baskets with scented plants near to the door or patio, where you'll be sitting, so that you can enjoy the fragrance. Sweet peas (for tumbling down), scented petunias and leaf-pelargoniums, low-growing flowering tobacco plants (*Nicotiana*), or a centrally planted cherry pie (*Heliotropium*). These can all generate some wonderful and evocative aromas.

ABOVE Plants such as the *Petunia* Surfinia – available in a range of whites, pinks, mauves and purples, as well as in double or single forms – can be planted singly within a hanging basket and, as long as they are watered and fed regularly throughout the growing season, will fill it with colour.

PLANTING A HANGING BASKET

1 Make sure your basket is stable. You can use its own chains to hang it from a greenhouse support or wall bracket, but it is often easier to remove the chains and pop it onto a large pot. Line the basket, either with a layer of moss, or a purpose-made shaped liner.

2 Place the liner in the basket, making sure it fits snugly. Pop a circle of plastic in the base to act as a water reserve. Begin filling your basket with soil-less compost (this is lighter). Check to see if it contains feed or water-retaining granules. If the basket allows you to plant through its sides, only fill it halfway for the moment.

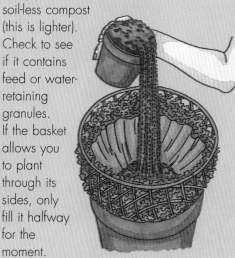

3 Large plants should go into the centre and smaller or trailing plants go at the edges. Cut holes in the liner if there aren't any, then gently push the rootball through the hole from the outside. If your compost does not have feed in it, add slow-release fertilizers.

4 Water the basket to settle in the plants. Until it is ready to go out, it is best to hang it in the greenhouse. Make sure to hang the basket securely.

WINDOWBOXES

These are ideal for bringing extra colour to a small garden. They can be rested on sills if those on the building are large enough, or they can be fixed to the wall below windows – although not, of course, in a position that will interfere with any windows that open outwards. Plastic boxes are available in various sizes and you can also buy sets consisting of the box, a water tray to avoid dripping, and the all-important brackets for fixing to the wall. The process of planting – which should be carried out after the box has been put into position and secured – is similar for that of pots and tubs.

Spring-flowering plants that are particularly appropriate to windowbox schemes include: *Crocus*, bedding double daisies (*Bellis*), shorter daffodils (*Narcissus*), dwarf wallflowers (*Erysimum*), forget-me-nots (*Myosotis*), grape hyacinths (*Muscari*), hyacinths (*Hyacinthus*), pansies (forms of *Viola*), polyanthus (forms of *Primula*) and tulips (*Tulipa*). And for summer: floss flower (*Ageratum*), shorter snapdragons (*Antirrhinum*), bedding begonias, busy lizzies (*Impatiens*), pinks and carnations (forms of *Dianthus*), bush and trailing *Fuchsia*, *Gazania*, upright and trailing *Pelargonium*, trailing *Lobelia*, bedding salvias, marigolds (forms of *Tagetes*) and *Petunia*.

Permanent plants, such as shrubs and perennials, are less successful in windowboxes because they tend to get rather large, and they are usually only at their best for a short period. When these plants are not 'in season', the windowbox will not be very attractive. Mostly when you see such woody plants as variegated ivies, *Hebe*, *Euonymus* and other dwarf conifers and evergreens, they are used more as temporary in-fills of foliage, particularly during the winter months when there is less colour to be had with flowering plants generally. These are also very hardy subjects so do not mind cold winter temperatures.

ABOVE A simple windowbox, with one type of plant (in this case small hybrid *Cyclamen* for winter colour) can look effective when the plants are established.

ABOVE This low trough for summer interest, which could become a windowbox if secured in the right way, contains the bright variegated foliage of *Iresine herbstii* 'Aureoreticulata' and deep beetroot-red shades of love-lies-bleeding (*Amaranthus caudatus*).

SUPPORTING AND PLANTING A WINDOWBOX

1 Unless you have a wide window ledge and either sash windows or casement windows that open inwards, you will have to set the box under the window. It is more attractive if you can use a box that spans the width of the window frame. To secure the box you will need to put up safety chains linked to hooks in either end of the box. Drill holes in the wall masonry 10in (25cm) up from the windowsill and about 4in (10cm) either side of the window frame. Insert wall plugs and screw in strong steel hooks. Normal wall brackets support the box from underneath.

2 If the window ledge can accommodate a box, but the ledge is not perfectly level, fix wedge-shaped pieces of wood (suitably treated with preservative) beneath the box, making sure these are sufficiently thick and spaced well apart. If you are unsure about the stability of the box, you can use several L-shaped brackets to screw the box to the ledge, or the wall, or even the window frame.

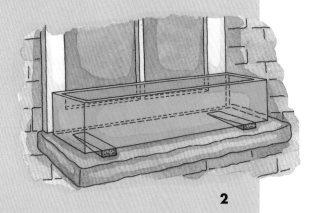

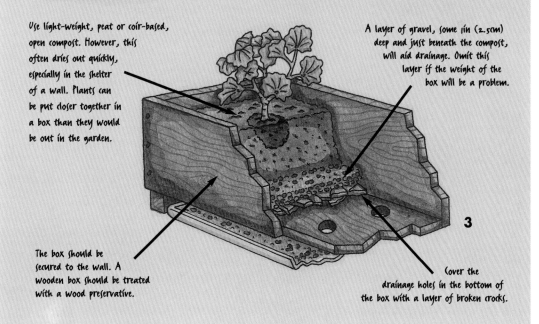

Use light-weight, peat or coir-based, open compost. However, this often dries out quickly, especially in the shelter of a wall. Plants can be put closer together in a box than they would be out in the garden.

A layer of gravel, some 1in (2.5cm) deep and just beneath the compost, will aid drainage. Omit this layer if the weight of the box will be a problem.

The box should be secured to the wall. A wooden box should be treated with a wood preservative.

Cover the drainage holes in the bottom of the box with a layer of broken crocks.

FRUIT AND VEGETABLES IN CONTAINERS

The range of food crops that can be grown in containers is wide, but some are easier to grow than others. If you have little available space for growing fruit trees, some smaller types can be grown in large tubs. There are two important provisos, however.

First, you should use as large a container as possible, and second, you should only grow a tree that has been grown on a 'dwarfing rootstock'. This means that the variety has been grafted on to special roots, which keep it dwarf (these trees are also often earlier fruiting).

RIGHT **Apple trees, on dwarfing rootstocks, are particularly suited to growing in containers. This 'Coronet' apple fruits well, and was specifically designed for tub cultivation.**

ABOVE **A wide range of vegetables and fruiting plants can be grown in containers — the only real limit you have is that of space.**

ABOVE **Onion is the ideal vegetable for a large tub – as plants requiring a small area in which to grow you can get lots of them in a single container.**

ABOVE **A group of fennel plants grow very contentedly in a sturdy container with a loam-based compost mix.**

ABOVE **A small hanging basket of parsley if hung next to the back door makes harvesting easy.**

Strawberries are ideal container plants, so much so that special strawberry barrels are available. These cylindrical plastic barrels are filled with compost and strawberry plants are set through holes in the sides and the top. I have even seen barrels on bases that rotate, so all plants can get some direct sunshine. Also, some barrels have a central tube for watering, and this is very useful as it helps ensure that water reaches the bottom of the barrel – this can be an unlikely occurrence in a well filled barrel that you water from the top; plants in the top half soak up the water before it can reach the plants lower down.

Some herbs such as parsley, tarragon, chives, rosemary, thyme and mint do well in containers too. In fact, I only ever grow mint (*Mentha*) in containers as all forms are vigorously invasive and will grow into other nearby plants. Growing them in a container keeps them under control. I have had great success also with a small hanging basket containing nothing but parsley – when hung next to the back door it made 'harvesting' very convenient.

The crops suggested for growing bags (see next page) are not difficult and can also be grown in tubs, hanging baskets and even windowboxes (for the smaller subjects).

GROWING BAGS

When growing bags were introduced in the 1970s it revolutionized tomato growing, and growing in containers generally. These are, quite simply, polythene bolsters of peat, coir, or recycled composted products, sometimes with sand or bark added. These days, too, you will often find that the compost in the bags has been impregnated with fertilizers to help the plants during the first few weeks, or pesticides to ward off the major insect pests (such as vine weevils), as well as the increasingly important water-saving gel granules.

Although growing bags are mainly used for cultivating tomatoes, they are also suitable for peppers, aubergines and cucumbers, plus hardier vegetables such as lettuce, onions, beetroot, radish and even French or dwarf beans. Strawberries do very well in growing bags, and there are many bulbs and bedding plants that will perform very well. Only woody plants and perennials are unsuitable. These bags can be placed outside in a sunny place, or can be sited in a greenhouse for early crops, or for very hot-loving (tropical) crops.

ABOVE In a typical growing bag you can plant three cordon tomatoes, but you will need either to invest in specially made growing bag supports, or you will have to rig up a system of canes and string.

ABOVE **Radishes are an ideal crop for a growing bag as they are small, and mature quickly.**

The planting process is very straightforward. Start by placing the bag into its permanent position: in a greenhouse or at the base of a sunny wall, and then cut it open. Most bags have printed on them the ideal places for making the cuts, and this will depend on whether you are growing tomatoes, peppers and aubergines (typically three plants per bag), cucumbers (two), or strawberries (six to eight).

Loosen the compost in the bag if it appears to be compacted, and water it if it seems to be dry. Remove the plants from their pots and plant them as evenly as possible along the centre of the bag. To stake the plants when in place, special supports are available for holding bamboo or plastic canes. These are essential for cordon and vine tomatoes (but not trailing tomatoes), aubergines, the larger types of pepper, and cucumbers. In fact, where greenhouse cucumbers are concerned you will need to tie something like pea and bean netting to the bag and to the roof of the greenhouse, and to allow the twining stems to grow through this. In the garden, the cucumber vines can be allowed to sprawl freely across the ground.

Maintaining growing bags throughout the season is not always as easy as it may seem at first, particularly as it can be difficult to tell when they need watering. The simplest test is to press a piece of newspaper on to the compost. If it picks up water the bag is moist enough. If not, a drink is needed!

Finally, a word about feeding in growing bags. As the vegetable crops are usually quite demanding in their nutrition intake, your involvement in providing food on a regular basis is vital. Indeed, it is not a bad idea to water the plants in with a weak solution of liquid feed when planting. Then for summer plants, a feed every week or 10 days is necessary as there are only limited supplies in the bag.

Use a tomato feed for all of the fruiting plants (including peppers, aubergines, cucumbers, strawberries and so on) as this contains slightly greater amounts of potash – for promoting flowers, and therefore fruits – than other fertilizers. A general fertilizer will be appropriate for all other plants. If you are growing spring plants or bulbs in growing bags, the fertilizer already within the bag is usually enough.

RAISED BEDS

Essentially these are no more than large, permanently sited containers. They can be made of ornamental stone, concrete blocks, bricks, or even old railway sleepers (available from specialist suppliers, usually listed in your local telephone directory).

The side wall of a raised bed, unlike a tall brick wall or the side of a building, does not usually need footings, or a foundation. However, these structures do retain an often heavy bank of soil, and you do not want them to collapse under the pressure. When I have constructed these in the past, I have dug a trench – some 4in (10cm) deep – along the line of where the wall will be, and into this trench I have poured a cement-concrete ready-mix. Smooth the surface and then water it lightly with a rosed watering can, and leave it overnight. The next day you will have a sturdy base, bonded to the surrounding soil onto which you can build your retaining wall. With this kind of footing, however, your wall should be no more than four courses deep.

LEFT **Raised beds can also be used for vegetables. This can be particularly useful for root crops, such as carrots, parsnips, potatoes and so on, which need a good depth of soil.**

ABOVE **Raised beds need not be tall affairs; even a two- or three-brick course will be sufficient to add height and interest to a garden.**

ABOVE **This raised bed in the author's garden was specially constructed to accommodate acid-loving plants (such as *Azalea*, *Erica* and *Camellia*) in what is an alkaline-soil garden.**

ABOVE **Raised beds can be made more 'rustic' if they have log edging fixed to the front. Unless the logs are treated and much longer (being set at least 18in [45cm]) below ground level), they will need a block wall behind them to support the weight of soil.**

The area within the raised bed should be dug over, and any weeds removed. Add well-rotted manure or compost as you go. In the past I have also added bought topsoil, as there was none available from anywhere else within the garden. To the topsoil, I added several bags of peat and ericaceous compost and created a bed for acid-loving plants in my mostly alkaline garden.

Similarly, if you wish to grow mainly alpine plants in your raised bed, you should add an extra part of coarse sand. Once the bed has been dug, weeded and filled with the appropriate soils and/or compost, water it well. Leave it for a day or two to settle and then you can begin to plant. The higher plants should be towards the centre of the bed, with the lower ones at the front and do not, of course, forget to grow a few trailing kinds to hang down the sides. Water all of the plants in well initially and then make sure to check for water regularly throughout the growing season.

ABOVE **A stone wall can be made to look natural, even though the blocks are mass produced and made of reconstituted stone.**

WATERING CONTAINER PLANTS

Plants in patio tubs, windowboxes and hanging baskets will need checking daily for water requirements – even twice daily in very hot weather – as they can dry out rapidly. Hanging baskets, especially, are notorious for this. Potted plants in these sorts of containers depend on us for all their needs, and since they can dry out within hours in summer, giving them a life-saving drink becomes a priority. The following are some effective watering methods to save you time and minimize water wastage.

ABOVE **It is important to get a good connector as the fitting between a hosepipe and a tap needs to be tight; there will be a considerable waste of water through drips otherwise. There are a number of connector types available from garden centres for any kind of tap.**

HOW TO WATER

The best way to water is with a watering can fitted with a rose spray, which distributes water evenly and so won't compact the compost. If you do not have a spray, place a piece of slate or old crock into the corner of the container, tilted downwards, and gently pour water on to it. This method prevents soil compaction and gives an even distribution of water. Ideally, repeat this in each corner.

WHEN TO WATER

Pot plants need watering all year round, except in freezing conditions. In winter, the rain may do it for you, but keep checking because foliage can act like an umbrella, or a wall can create a dry spot. Water in the early morning or evening when evaporation rates are at their lowest. By mid-summer, hanging baskets are full of plants and use a lot of water. Even worse, they tend to hang by sunny walls, and the heat that the walls reflect makes them dry out even more. So anything that you can do to keep them moist is worthwhile. Watering twice a day may well be necessary in summer.

Growing bags, too, will increasingly be demanding water as the bags become filled with root, and the crops that are full of moisture (tomatoes, cucumbers, peppers and aubergines particularly) will be sucking up every bit of available water. In a sun trap outdoors, the bags may need watering twice a day. Use rainwater from a water butt for watering mature container plants; but use tap water for seedlings and young, tender plants (which are more delicate, and prone to infection from the impurities and bacteria present in rainwater).

ABOVE **Watering equipment manufacturers have designed hooked lance attachments for connecting to hosepipes for watering hanging baskets that are placed too high to reach normally.**

USING WATER-RETAINING GEL

Mix polymer granules (widely available) with the compost at planting time; follow the directions on the granule packet. These dry granules absorb moisture and turn into a gel, swelling to many times their own weight. They release moisture to plants over many months and even seasons. Plants that benefit most from such gels are those that grow rapidly and are planted in light, open compost (such as peat- or coir-based composts), from which moisture quickly evaporates.

KEEP EXPOSED CONTAINERS MOIST

In hot summer winds containers (particularly hanging baskets and sun-drenched windowboxes) dry out more quickly. It is essential to use the retaining gels in these for a constant supply of moisture. Also, invest in a special extension hose and hooked watering lance so that you do not have to hold up heavy watering cans. With these also you will be able to direct water to where it is needed more easily.

AUTOMATIC WATERING SYSTEMS

These are expensive and can be cumbersome to install, but they are very effective. They are also water-efficient, and are particularly useful when you are absent. You set the times when the system starts and stops, and in the more sophisticated versions you can even determine how much water is used. All you need is an outside tap and an adjacent area where plants can be lined up.

RESCUING DRIED-OUT POTS

If the compost in the pot has shrunk, add a few drops of washing-up liquid to the water in your can to help re-wet it. For badly wilted plants, stand the dried-out container in a bowl of water and place it in the shade for an hour or two; then remove from the bowl. If a plant collapses before you can get to watering it, submerge the pot in a bucket of water until no more bubbles escape, then remove and leave it in the shade.

AFTERCARE FOR CONTAINER PLANTS

◆ Remove all dead flowers and yellowing leaves as they appear.
◆ Feed every week with a general liquid fertilizer.
◆ Keep an eye out for pests and diseases, such as greenfly, blackfly and whitefly, vine weevil, caterpillars, slugs and snails, and treat as necessary.
◆ If a tub is near to a wall, and in the case of all hanging baskets, turn them regularly, otherwise all the flowers will all appear on just one side.
◆ Finally, make sure that any pottery (terracotta, earthenware or ceramic) pots that are kept outdoors over the winter are frost-resistant or 'frost hardy'. If not they will crack and shatter after one or two bad frosts.

ABOVE **If you have a great many containers and/or you are absent often, it is a good idea to install some form of automatic watering system. A main hose is connected to a tap with a timer device; coming from this main pipe are small feeder pipes which are inserted, via pegs or spikes, into individual pots.**

CHAPTER 6

Trees, shrubs and border plants

rees and shrubs – together these are the backbone of any garden. They should be the first plants put into a bare garden; the border plants (perennials, alpines, bulbs, annuals, biennials and roses), although crucial in their own right, should really only be planned in to a garden once the trees and shrubs have been accommodated. Let's look at each of the different plant groups as they apply to the water-saving garden, what to look for when buying them, and then how to get them planted.

ABOVE Trees and shrubs, such as this blue *Ceanothus* and yellow *Potentilla*, are the backbone of a garden.

TREES, SHRUBS AND CLIMBERS

The majority of these, when bought from garden centres and shops, are already growing in pots, and they do have many advantages over 'bare-root' plants (that is, plants that have been lifted from a nursery bed or field situation where they were growing in the ground). The main advantage is that they can be planted not only in winter, but throughout the year.

When hunting for woody plants at the garden centre do not be swayed by a colourful flower display. Look at the plants closely to determine their states of health. Make sure the stems are healthy and strong, and that the plants are not obviously diseased or damaged in any way. Try also to make sure that the plants are genuine container-grown plants, not bare-root specimens that have recently been potted up, perhaps hurriedly, for the nursery or garden centre to

ABOVE **Variegated shrubs, such as this** *Elaeagnus pungens* 'Goldrim', **always perform best when grown in full sun.**

ABOVE **Spring-flowering shrubs (such as** *Cytisus* x *praecox* 'Allgold') **can be grown to complement bulbs blooming at the same time (here is** *Narcissus* 'Salome').

ABOVE **Some shrubs (such as the false castor oil plant, *Fatsia japonica*, with hand-shaped leaves) have an 'architectural' quality in the garden.**

ABOVE **The majority of trees, shrubs and conifers bought from garden centres these days are sold already growing in containers.**

make a quick sale and get rid of them. You can tell if shrubs have been in their containers for the proper length of time by moss or algae on the soil surface – although an excess of this can also indicate lax practices in the nursery, where plant

hygiene (that is, weeding and pest and diseases control) have been less than rigorous. Another way to identify how long a plant has been in a pot is to see if the roots are beginning to push through the holes in the base of the container. Most importantly, however, you should ask! If you go to a reliable nursery, the staff there should be able to give you accurate and informative advice.

'BARE-ROOT' PLANTS

Most are destined for sale in smaller plant nurseries, the thriving mail order plant businesses and in stores and supermarkets. In the case of the latter two, these bare-root plants are pre-packed and sealed, usually with some moisture kept around the roots by packing in moist tissue paper, or a small amount of compost. If you really know what you are looking for, it is possible to get excellent plants in this way, and they are usually cheaper than container-grown types because you are not buying the pot and soil. You also have the advantage of seeing if the plant has a well-developed root system.

Watch out, however, for those with dried-up stems, or with premature growth caused by high temperatures, where the transparent packaging has created a mini 'greenhouse' around the plants. Also, avoid specimens with spindly little shoots, or any that are discoloured with disease. Saleable plants should have a good, fibrous root system and a minimum of two strong, firm shoots, no thinner than a pencil, and preferably thicker. Late autumn is the best time to plant bare-root trees, shrubs and climbers although they are generally available for much of the year.

For the vast majority of trees, shrubs and climbers the soil needs to be free-draining, but also moisture-retentive. This sounds like it is a contradiction, but in fact most soils do have these joint qualities (see pages 28–37).

ABOVE **Bare-root trees, shrubs and roses should be soaked in water for an hour or so before they are planted; this will stimulate some of the drier roots into growth.**

CONTAINER-GROWN PLANTS

Trees, shrubs or climbers sold in containers can be planted at any time of year, but if you are planting during the summer, or during a period of hot weather in spring or autumn, you must make sure to check for watering, almost on a daily basis, until the soil is consistently moist.

Just because container-grown plants have a neat root-ball when removed from the pot, do not be fooled into thinking that you simply need to dig a hole the same size as the root-ball, and then to drop it in. If you did this on a heavy clay soil you would be inadvertently creating a sump from which water would be slow to drain, and this could cause the roots to rot. It is a good idea, therefore, to break up the surrounding soil, and the base of the hole at planting time. Firm the plant in position, and water it in.

STAKING AND FEEDING

A stake should be used to support small trees and it should be driven into the hole before planting, so as to avoid damaging the roots.

The top of the stake should come up just to the base of the first outward branches, to avoid unnecessary rubbing. Just before you place any plants into the ground, apply a dressing of bonemeal fertilizer over the area at the rate of 2oz per sq yd (65g per m²). Work it into the surface of the soil, using a hoe or rake to tread the area firm, and then rake it level.

CLIMBING PLANTS

These require a little extra attention. Setting a climbing plant against a wall usually requires you to plant it 12in (30cm) or so away from the wall, in order to avoid the footings. In this case, make the hole and lay the plant at an angle, with the above-ground part of the plant leaning slightly towards the wall. If it is a bare-root specimen, point the roots away from the wall (where the soil will usually be drier), and towards moister soil. Water the climber in, and check it regularly for the first year, particularly during hot weather.

CIRCLE OF SOIL

When trees are planted in areas of grass it is absolutely essential that a circle of soil – a minimum of 3ft (1m) in diameter – at the base of the stem be maintained for several years, at least until the tree is well established. Not only does this circle of soil allow easy access of water to the roots it also removes the need for grass cutters to approach too close to the stem. Many serious wounds to tree bark are caused by attempts to cut grass growing around the base of tree stems.

The circle must be kept free of weeds and rubbish, and it is best if you can weed this area by hand. By all means hoe the circle to remove weeds if you have to, but if you nick some tree roots near the soil surface, you may encourage suckers. To prevent the soil in the circle from drying out during hot spells, a 2in (5cm) mulch of grass mowings, compost, manure or leafmould may be applied, taking care to keep the base of the stem clear. It also pays to check newly planted trees after periods of frost when the roots become loosened and the soil lifted. Simply re-firm the soil with your foot, but do this after the ground has thawed.

ABOVE **Make the circle by putting a peg into the ground, attached to which is a line equal in length to the radius of the desired circle. Attach another peg to the end of the line and 'scrape' in arcs across the turf to form the circle.**

ABOVE **The finished circle of soil in the grass. This permits better water penetration around the roots during a period of rain or when being irrigated and means that you will not need to use a grass cutter close to the trunk.**

PERENNIALS, ALPINES, FERNS AND ORNAMENTAL GRASSES

Although not woody, all of these plants will survive and provide you with colour and interest from year to year. In most cases after four or five years it would be recommended that you lift them out of the ground and split, or divide them, and then to replant the healthiest and most vigorous portions. This not only stops the plant from getting too large and cumbersome, but

also gives it a new lease of life. Division in this way is also a form of propagation, so from one 'mother' plant you could end up with anything from two to twenty plants, depending on what it is and how big it has become.

Perennials are generally grown in pots in the nursery, and this is how you buy them. Always buy the best plants you can find. Look for

ABOVE **Perennials, such as lupins and hostas seen here, provide you with colour and interest from year to year, but these plants do die down to nothing every winter.**

69

ABOVE Blue gentians, pink rhodohypoxis and white saxifrages are wonderful plants for the rockery or alpine garden – but really they are just small perennials needing a well-drained soil.

vigorous, healthy specimens; they should also be young, as these will tend to establish and grow away quickly. You should not, however, buy the largest plants you see necessarily: these may be pot bound and will take time to establish. If you do end up buying a perennial plant that is pot bound, at planting time gently tease out as many of the roots from the congested 'ball' of root as possible, but try not to damage them too much. Ideally, perennials should be planted in the spring or autumn; early-flowering subjects (such as forms of *Helleborus*, *Bergenia*, *Hepatica* and some forms of *Primula*) are best planted in the autumn so that they have a chance to settle in before flowering.

Water the plants in their pots thoroughly an hour or two before planting them so that the plant has plenty of moisture in its system in advance of the 'shock' of having its roots exposed to the air and possibly become damaged – even if this is

ABOVE **For each plant, dig a hole that is large enough to accommodate the entire root system.**

ABOVE **With perennials you should always buy the best quality plants you can find, but do not necessarily buy the largest plants you see, as they may be pot bound, and it will take them a long time to establish in the soil.**

just for a matter of seconds. This is especially important during hot, dry, or windy weather. For each plant, dig a hole that is large enough to accommodate the entire root system. Depending on the size of the plant this may require the use of a trowel or a spade. Carefully remove the plant from its container and, if possible, spread out the roots as you place the plant in the hole. Set the crown of the plant at soil level, then back fill, firm and water in the plant.

PLANTING A BRAND NEW BORDER

If the border is devoid of plants, and you have a sort of 'blank canvas', it is a good idea to set out the plants whilst they are still in their pots. This will give you an idea of what the eventual display will look like (although you will need a little imagination to visualize them when fully grown). Most plant labels that come with your purchases give dimensions of height and spread when the plants are fully grown, and it is important to take note of these. You can then improve the spacings and placings accordingly. It is all too easy to plant perennials too close to each other, which can encourage weak and spindly growth, and make the plants more susceptible to attack by fungal diseases.

BULBOUS PLANTS

To most people flowering bulbs are the spring-flowering daffodils (*Narcissus*), tulips, crocuses, hyacinths and so on. But you can choose bulbs so that there is something in flower right through the year. The types that flower in winter and in early spring include snowdrops (*Galanthus*) and winter aconites (*Eranthis*). In summer there are lilies, *Gladiolus* and *Dahlia*. In the autumn there are *Colchicum*, *Schizostylis* and *Sternbergia*.

As for buying bulbs, mid-summer is when the first of the new season's mail order bulb catalogues are published. Although the following spring may seem, and is, a long way off, ordering early has many advantages: those that require early planting, such as colchicums and daffodils will be with you in good time; also, if you delay ordering, some varieties may be sold out later in the season. The range of bulbs available by mail order is extensive and includes unusual varieties.

Mail-ordered bulbs will be selected at the nursery, so in terms of bulb quality, you are stuck with what you are sent – but do not be afraid to complain or send the bulbs back if they turn out to be substandard. From mid-summer onwards bulbs will also be on display at garden centres, and these offer you the opportunity to browse, choose, and plan your display. Much useful information about colour, height and growing is to be found on accompanying point of sale material. There are a number of important points to remember when selecting bulbs from a shop. Avoid any that do not have a clean base, or are soft and show signs of rot, or have started to shoot, producing more than a very small amount of growth. This applies especially to daffodils and hyacinths. Select plump, firm well-rounded examples. Lily bulbs should be fleshy and firm, here again avoid any that are dried out. Larger bulbs usually result in the finest flower spikes.

ABOVE Hyacinths are an archetypal spring-flowering bulb (along with daffodils, tulips, crocuses and so on); this is *Hyacinthus* 'Pink Royal'.

In the spring many summer-flowering bulbs and tubers will be on sale, the same rules of buying apply. Store bulbs in a cool dry place, never near heaters – and never in plastic bags as this makes them sweat. Open any bags before planting to let air circulate. Daffodils are frequently offered for naturalizing (planting out to look like a 'natural' drift of colour, usually in a grassed area), and these are often sold in large bags. These will contain a mixture of varieties and at a competitive price. Alternatively, you can usually make your own selection of bulbs from large bins.

PLANTING BULBS

Plant out the bulbs as soon as possible. Textbooks often quote very specific depths for bulbs when they are planted. As a general rule, however, a bulb should be planted so that there is as much soil above it as the height of the bulb itself; you will not go far wrong with this. Exceptions are bluebells and daffodils, which should be planted twice their own depth.

The spring-flowering bulbs are the first to be planted during the 'bulb year' and these should go in during the autumn. Daffodils and other forms of *Narcissus* could be planted in late summer or beginning of autumn, as they produce roots early. The majority of bulbs, with the exception of tulips, can be planted as soon as the summer bedding has been removed or when the ground is vacant. In the case of tulips they should be planted from mid-autumn onwards; these require a shorter period in the ground before they start to grow, and if they shoot too early any emerging new growth may be damaged by frost. Summer-flowering bulbs, such as gladioli and dahlias, are planted in spring. These two, and many other types of summer bulb, are tender and will need lifting or

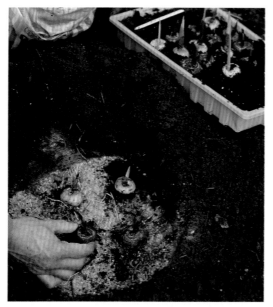

ABOVE **Summer-flowering bulbs (and corms such as *Gladiolus*, seen here), are planted in spring; the tender types will need lifting again in the autumn as winter wet and cold can cause the corms to rot.**

ABOVE **Lily bulbs are usually much larger than all other bulbs; they can be planted into pots as well as out in the border, where they appreciate conditions from full sun to dappled shade.**

RIGHT **A bulb planter is inserted into the ground, and when it is pulled out it brings a plug of soil with it. The bulb is placed into the hole, and then the plug of soil is replaced. These tools can be used in the border, but are perhaps even more useful when planting bulbs into the harder soil of a lawn.**

trowels; these have a long narrow blade with measurements marked on it that guide you to the appropriate depth. If you are planting bulbs in grass, a hand-held bulb planter is helpful, this removes a plug of soil when pushed into the ground. The bulb is inserted into the hole and the plug replaced. It is a much quicker method of planting when large numbers of bulbs need to be planted at one time.

Always ensure the base of the bulb is in contact with the ground. Air pockets result in the roots failing to develop. Unless you are planning formal beds, plant in groups; this is much more effective. Some people may be allergic to handling daffodils, tulips and hyacinth bulbs; they can cause a rash on the skin. If in doubt use gloves. Finally, do not forget to mark the area, perhaps with a visible plant label of some description; planted bulbs are hidden from view, and it is easy to walk over the area and damage the emerging shoots.

otherwise protecting in the winter. Lilies can be set out in the autumn. Most gardeners use an ordinary trowel for planting bulbs. However, you can also buy special graduated bulb-planting

ABOVE **Many types of bulb, but predominately forms of daffodil, can be grown in areas of grass, a style of growing called 'naturalizing'.**

BEDDING PLANTS (VARIOUS ANNUALS AND BIENNIALS)

Annuals are plants that are sown, grow, flower and die all within a year, whereas biennials are sown and grown on in one year, and flower and die during a second year. Bedding plants is the term used to describe plants of either type, but generally grown in quantity, and planted in 'beds', for a massed display. These include the fibrous-rooted bedding begonia (*Begonia semperflorens*), sweet williams (*Dianthus barbatus*), foxgloves (*Digitalis purpureus*) and polyanthus (hybrids of *Primula* x *polyantha*).

At the garden centre or shop, bedding plants are sold in trays or pots and, depending on the type, are available from six months before they are due to flower, right up until they have already started to flower. Look for healthy specimens: there should be no weeds, or pests or diseases present. And the ideal plant will not yet have started to flower, which will mean that you have a full season of colour ahead of you.

ABOVE **French marigolds (this is *Tagetes* 'Disc Flame') make a spectacle of colour in summer beds and borders, but they are not to everyone's taste.**

ABOVE **Bedding begonias (*Begonia semperflorens* hybrids) make a wonderful show of colour in the summer months.**

ABOVE **Foxgloves (generally forms of *Digitalis purpurea*) are** biennials: seed is sown in the summer, the seedlings from which grow and overwinter, for flowering the following summer, after which they die.

ABOVE **Snapdragons (*Antirrhinum*) are annual – or tender perennial** – bedding plants and come in a range of colours from yellow, orange, red and pink, through to white.

If they have already started blooming the plants will have developed a significant root system and may respond badly when planted out. You will also have missed some of the flowering potential. If the plants you desire have all started to flower whilst still on the shop's shelves, the aim should be to go for the trays, or plants, with the fewest flowers.

PLANTING BEDDING PLANTS

Most annual types will be tender (in that they will be damaged by frost or very cold weather). So these plants, which will have been started into growth in a greenhouse, will need very slow acclimatization in spring to colder conditions – a term known as 'hardening off'. They should not, of course, be fully planted out in the garden or in containers until all danger of frosts has passed.

The soil in which they are to grow should be prepared well, as this can affect the performance of the plants during their short lives most directly. Before planting, fork the soil over, making sure that any annual weeds are completely buried. Perennial weeds however should be removed as these will re-grow if left. To feed the bedding plants through the season, apply a sprinkling of general fertilizer evenly over the soil, following the manufacturer's instructions. An hour or two before planting, give the plants a thorough watering. If the bedding plants are in individual pots, gently removed them and place them in a hole dug with a trowel.

If the plants are in plastic or polystyrene strips, you will need to either break the strips apart, or gently tease the plants out of their compartments. In each case, try to do as little damage to the roots and stems as possible. Damaged leaves will readily be replaced with new leaves, within reason, but a plant only has one stem! The hole should be slightly larger than the plant's root-ball. Drop the root-ball in and firm it in place with your hands. Then water it in and put a label in position if you wish to remember what's what.

ABOVE **Petunias (this is 'Junior Crystal Red') excel in a position in full sun; many forms have highly scented flowers.**

ABOVE **When looking for bedding plants at the garden centre try not to buy trays or multi-packs if the plants are already in full flower.**

ROSES

The quintessential English rose is, actually, a universal flower; forms of roses come from most continents. A garden that does not contain at least a couple in some form or other is, in my view, sadly lacking. A good quality bush, miniature, or ground-cover rose should normally have between three and five stems, each neatly pruned back by the nursery where it was growing to 10–18in (25–45cm) in length. The root-balls should be well furnished with main and fibrous roots.

Climbers and ramblers should have two or more stems, each at least 30in (45cm) long. The stems should be green and clean, and buds should be dormant. Long, pale green or white shoots from the stems should not be present. Avoid any roses that appear to have suckers, which weaken the whole plant, and any plant that is lopsided, with roots concentrated on one side only. Avoid container-grown roses where the compost level is far above or below the graft point (or 'union') at the stem base. There are far too many container roses that appear as if on stilts, with the compost washed away from the roots. Finally, as with any container-grown plants, there should be minimal amounts of moss or weed growth on the compost itself.

If your soil is extremely sandy, and does not hold water well, you must incorporate plenty of humus into it before planting. Mix it well into the soil around and within the planting hole; do not plant a rose right into this material as it is too strong for the fine root hairs and will burn them. And if your soil is heavy clay, bulky organic matter as described should be used to break up the soil; to aid drainage, and provide valuable nutrition to what is likely to be an impoverished soil.

If you live in a high chalk area, where, say, there is a maximum topsoil layer of 18in (45cm) or so before you get to the chalk layer, you will

ABOVE **The rose is the quintessential 'English' flower, although they are found the world over; this is the hybrid tea 'Tequila Sunrise'.**

ABOVE **When planting roses, the soil around the roots should contain a mix of peat, coir or other open 'bulky organic matter'; this helps the roots to establish.**

have difficulty in growing roses. You could opt to grow only the lime-tolerant types, mainly the Alba, Damask and Hybrid Musk shrub roses. Alternatively you could import a 2ft (60cm) depth of new, suitable topsoil. Or, with your normal soil you could dig a much bigger planting hole, some 2ft (60cm) or deeper, and also incorporate a generous quantity of tree and shrub planting mixture (bagged loam and organic material available from garden retailers). Roses are at their absolute best in the sun, and will only do really well if they have it for most of the day.

PLANTING ROSES

Just before you set the plants in the ground, apply a dressing of bonemeal fertilizer over the area at the rate of 2oz per sq yd (65g per m²). Work it into the surface of the soil, using a hoe or rake, tread the area firm, and then rake it

ABOVE **Floribunda roses (this is 'Agatha Christie') are usually slightly taller than the hybrid teas. All roses prefer growing in a sunny position and in a moist, fertile soil.**

level. Start the actual planting by digging the hole. The soil from it should be mixed with a shop-bought planting mixture, or you can make your own by mixing soil with peat or peat-substitute, and a handful of slow-release fertilizer. This mixture should be kept in a pile next to the hole.

ABOVE **Bring the soil back into the hole around the rootball.**

ABOVE **Firm the rose into its position; use your foot to 'tread' the plant in place, but be careful not to trample on it, or to damage the roots.**

ABOVE **Water the rose in. You will need to check for water and apply it as required for at least the first year of the plant's life.**

The hole itself should be deep enough for the budding union of the rose (that is, the point when the plant is budded on to the rootstock) to be about 1in (2.5cm) below soil level. In the case of bare-root roses the hole should be wide enough for the roots to fan out as evenly as possible all round, if they grow that way. Many roses have all their roots pointing in one direction and these should be placed at one side of the planting hole, not in the middle, and the roots then spread out as widely as you can. Hold the rose in position, replace the planting mixture over the roots and gently shake the plant so that the mixture falls down either between the roots or to the side of the root-ball. Fill with more of the mixture, and then tread firmly, but not too hard, around the roots without damaging them.

Replace all the soil, firm with your foot again, and level the area off. Then apply at least one, preferably two, watering cans of water to help the roots establish.

Standard roses need a relatively shallow hole, just enough for the roots to be covered. If they are more deeply planted, the rootstocks, which are usually taken from *Rosa rugosa*, will sucker freely. A stake should always support a standard rose, and it should be driven into the hole before planting, so as to avoid damaging the plant's roots. The top of the stake should come up just to the budding union, which in standards is just beneath the head of branches. Plant a climber rose as you would any other woody climbing plant (see Trees, shrubs and climbers, above).

ROSE 'SICKNESS'

If you are planting new roses into a bed that already has had roses in it for a long time, the soil is likely to be 'rose-sick'. Due to a build-up of soil parasites and a depletion of mineral reserves, newly planted roses may not do at all well, even if the previous plants have appeared reasonably healthy.

The answer is to change the top 12–15in (30–38cm) of soil, or to sterilize it chemically. You may even opt to plant the roses elsewhere, using instead the previous rose bed for other plants. To change the soil, dig out the top layer, to the depth stated, and exchange it with soil from, say, the vegetable garden or an empty border. Or, if you have the capacity within your garden to accommodate extra volume, buy in some new, clean topsoil from a supplier. Before replacing the fresh soil in the rose bed, dig over the bottom and empty in a good layer of rotted organic matter. Allow the replaced soil to settle naturally during the winter before planting.

To sterilize the soil dig the bed over to a depth of 12in (30cm), while the soil is still fairly warm, in early autumn, adding a good layer of well-rotted organic matter. Then apply a soil sterilant at the maker's recommended dosage, then cover the area with polythene for four or five weeks to retain the fumes so they have time to act in the soil.

ABOVE **Rose 'sickness' disease can affect new roses on a site that previously had roses growing on it. To help prevent the disease, replace the soil with new soil (from a different part of the garden, or newly bought-in topsoil), and incorporate plenty of bulky organic matter, such as well-rotted garden compost.**

WATERING TREES, SHRUBS AND OTHER BORDER PLANTS

Trees and shrubs are, without doubt, the thirstiest of the garden's network of permanent plants. Just think about a mature 60ft (18m) tree and how it needs to absorb huge amounts of water to fill all of its growing cells – every day. As we have already seen in this book, leaves transpire moisture, and just look at how many leaves a tree of this size may have: it could be a million or more.

The good news, however, is that a tree of this size will usually be able to look after itself. Its roots will penetrate far and deep, and will tap into the water table. The most crucial period for a tree to be given supplementary water, however, is during the first few years after planting. Watering at planting time settles the soil particles around the roots, enabling newly developed root hairs to take up water. Roots of bare-root trees will take time to develop and

search out water, so adequate supply needs to be on hand as the new leaf canopy develops and the tree demands increasingly more water.

Perennials and bedding plants will usually appreciate quite a bit of supplementary watering during hot weather; the bedding plants usually showing signs of dehydration before the perennials. If the bed or border is densely planted a sprinkler may be employed to good effect, but make sure that the water spray does not land on uncultivated ground for this would be a serious waste of water. Bulbous plants tend to have their own reserves of moisture stored within the bulb. The few fleshy roots that emit from the base of the bulbs are there to absorb supplementary soil moisture when the bulbs start to get dry. Watering growing bulbs in hot weather can be advantageous, but do not overwater them as this can readily cause rotting.

ABOVE **When watering, give priority to the newly planted kinds – and avoid watering during the heat of the day when evaporation will be at its most significant.**

81

CHAPTER 7

Gardening under cover

The greenhouse (which many gardeners have) along with polytunnels, frames and perhaps a series of cloches (which many dedicated gardeners have), are all places where heavy demands on water are made. Then there is also the conservatory. These days a conservatory, usually attached and connected to the house, is kept for entertaining and 'living', rather than a centre for growing and nurturing plants – the original purpose of conservatories. However, any plant growing in a conservatory will be subjected to the same extremes of temperature and potential dryness as a plant growing underneath the other forms of cover mentioned. Let's look at the various structures in turn.

ABOVE A greenhouse gives us an entirely new dimension to our gardening; here you can see how even a small greenhouse in early spring can be used to propagate and nurture a range of plants.

ABOVE The same greenhouse can be used as a 'display house' during the summer months. Here, there are a number of annuals and exotic plants growing in pots.

THE GREENHOUSE AND THE POLYTUNNEL

If you find yourself gazing miserably across a soggy garden on a wintery or rainy day, invest in a greenhouse and potter away to your heart's content regardless of the conditions outside. There are small versions that can be tucked away in an odd corner – as long as it is not in heavy shade – and most gardens have a suitable spot. A greenhouse need not be an eyesore either. You do not want them to be 'plonked' in place, and to stand out like a sore thumb, so why not fence them off, or design flowerbeds or borders around them so that they become an integral part of the garden.

Polytunnels tend to be more for the person with a large garden or even a smallholding.

These are, it has to be said, not attractive structures; however, they do permit growing slightly tender plants in quantity. With either of these structures you will be able to:

1 Bring certain plants on to flower or fruit earlier than if they were outside.
2 Propagate plants by seed or cutting – which could save you a fortune in the long term.
3 Protect, overwinter and nurture a range of tender plants that would perish outside. With the tender plants you will just need to make sure that in the winter there is some form of heating, or at least good insulation against the glass, to keep in the day's warmth.

ABOVE **Cheapness and ease of erection are the chief advantages of a polytunnel. The tubular steel frame is easily put together and a one-piece polythene 'envelope' fits over it. No foundations are necessary, for the ends of the polythene are buried in the ground for anchorage.**

ABOVE **Even a small greenhouse without heating can be used to house tender plants during the winter months. This young olive tree (*Olea europaea*) would have suffered outside during the coldest weather.**

RIGHT **A greenhouse needs shading in the summer, otherwise during sunny spells plants inside can burn to a crisp – even with adequate watering and ventilation.**

PROPAGATION

The real benefit of owning a greenhouse or polytunnels is that you can propagate your own plants. For me there is so much pleasure in sowing seeds from a packet, and then seeing the green shoots emerging after a few days or weeks. For at least six months of the year there are flower and vegetable seeds you could sow to give you plenty to enjoy. Later in the year you can sow seeds of biennials and perennials that will give you something to look at next year.

You can also propagate cuttings in a greenhouse. Healthy shoot tips of trees, shrubs, conifers and perennials can be given their first stirrings of new life in a greenhouse. Some will be more difficult to encourage to root than others; some will need a sand-base to grow in, some will need a bit of heat, and most will enjoy regular misting over with water (see Watering Under Cover, below)… but having the greenhouse in the first place is the important thing.

In early autumn, many semi-hardwood evergreen cuttings will root in pots or trays placed on the bench in a greenhouse or polytunnel. If possible these should be placed well away from doors and windows and, provided they are kept moist, rooting will take place over the winter months and new growth will begin in early to mid-spring. Rooting will be more successful if the cuttings are prevented from freezing either by heating the greenhouse or by covering the pots during cold periods. In bright periods, particularly in early spring, the cuttings must be shaded to prevent them being scorched.

Hardwood cuttings, even those of easier subjects such as willows and many dogwoods, will benefit from being rooted under the protection of a greenhouse where the cuttings can be left in a shady corner in deep trays or pots. Polytunnels tend to retain more moisture than a greenhouse, and are therefore ideal for rooting cuttings. However, the still, humid atmosphere can cause problems with diseases such as grey mould, particularly in the winter months. Three ways to reduce the risk of grey mould infection are to:

1 Increase ventilation by opening vents or end panels making sure you close them at night.

2 Space the cuttings further apart, again to improve air circulation.

3 To promptly remove dead leaves.

THE GARDEN FRAME

A garden frame is ideal for raising many types of tree or shrub seed, and for rooting most types of cutting and can be easier to manage than a greenhouse where the environment has to be a compromise to suit a range of different requirements. Wooden-sided frames are more suitable for cuttings than those with metal or glass sides; the wooden sides help to keep a more even temperature and only the top needs to be shaded from the sun. Ideally the frame should be placed on a paved or concrete base, and in a position out of the midday sun.

To ensure good drainage you should put a layer of gravel in the bottom of the frame. If the frame lid fits well, pots of semi-hardwood cuttings can be placed directly into the frame. Pots of softwood cuttings will benefit from being placed either under individual covers or in a propagator. Alternatively, the whole of the frame can be filled with cuttings compost to a depth of 4–6in (10–15cm) and the cuttings inserted directly into the frame. This is ideal for evergreen semi-hardwood and hardwood cuttings, which can be inserted into the frame in autumn and lifted the following year.

It is important during periods of bright sunlight to make sure that the frame is shaded, even during late autumn and early spring. A piece of shade netting, which can be draped over the top of the frame, is ideal as it can be easily removed. Avoid using the shade-whitening products used for painting onto greenhouses as these are permanent and can cause elongated growth if dull weather coincides with the start of shoot development.

ABOVE Garden frames need not be obtrusive; here a couple of 'Dutch light'-style coldframes are all but hidden behind a row of tomatoes growing outside. It is important, however, to place frames where they will receive good levels of sunshine.

ABOVE This modern aluminium garden frame is tall enough to accommodate pepper plants; it is more like a mini-greenhouse in effect.

85

THE CLOCHE

Several centuries ago, the French were using small glass domes or 'bell jars' to protect plants in the open during the colder months of the year. A variation of them, the cloche, took the French word for 'bell' as its name, and became a mainstay in gardens throughout most of the past 100 years. There are numerous benefits of using cloches, but essentially the main benefit is the cultivation of earlier crops. A row of cloches will bring you succulent early strawberries and a continuous supply of winter lettuce. If your garden is exposed, glass cloches can even be used – if placed on their ends as a sort of windbreak – to protect slightly tender plants, such as tomatoes.

ABOVE **Wire hoops at regular intervals support a polythene tunnel cloche. Ventilation and harvesting of crops is made simple, by easily pulling up the polythene sides.**

The simplest form of cloche is a mini polytunnel made from wire hoops and a stretch of polythene to go over them. Such a device can cover just a single row of vegetables in a kitchen garden or allotment, but can work wonders at bringing them on early. Certain cloches are offered for sale that are described as 'self-

ABOVE **This single strip of rigid corrugated plastic is one of the simplest styles of modern cloche.**

watering'. This usually means that they have a flat roof panel that collects rain or irrigation water and allows it to drip through on to the plants and soil. Only personal experience will reveal the effectiveness of this, but there are two possible disadvantages. The first is the constant gap in the glass that, although allowing ventilation, may make for premature loss of heat. And the second is that dripping of water on to the plants may create the perfect conditions for fungal diseases, such as botrytis, to get a hold.

ABOVE **The traditional glass 'barn' cloche can have high- and low-sided versions; it offers plenty of room for one row of larger vegetables, or for two rows of more modest-sized crops.**

THE FEATURES OF A GOOD CLOCHE

◆ Durability and mobility. The great advantage of cloches should be their ease of mobility. Pick a type which you can move around without doing yourself damage! Their ability to resist wind is also important. Plastic or polycarbonate is supple but relatively short-lived; glass is rigid but brittle.

◆ Ease of erection. The earliest cloches involved two or four panes of glass (not three) and fairly complicated wire clips. It was a palaver putting the thing together. These days pre-moulded cloches of polycarbonate construction can be simply dropped into place.

◆ Ventilation. All cloches should have ventilation facilities, whether this involves propping up the sides with a brick or adjusting a pane of glass.

◆ Good light transmission. Both glass and plastic/polycarbonate will admit plenty of light, but you should avoid those types that have a bulky, shade-casting frame.

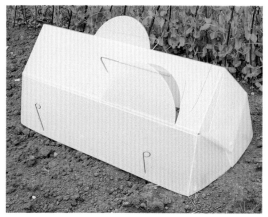

ABOVE **Small individual cloches, made from Perspex and with opening panels for ventilation are available today.**

ABOVE **This cloche is made from horticultural fleece, stretched taut between wire hoops. It provides shading as well as weather protection to the crops underneath.**

THE CONSERVATORY

Those of us who are lucky enough to have a conservatory know only too well how much they can add to our homes. They make great additional living space: from a luxurious dining room with an all-round view of the garden, to a place for hiding away and curtaining off children's toys. But you are being unfair to yourself if you have a conservatory and do not grow a few plants in it. With just a little effort you could create a mini version of the world-famous Palm House at the Royal Botanic Gardens at Kew, near London – conservatories are perfect places to grow many of our tender plants. The structure allows enough light in to make many plants believe they are outdoors, yet it protects them from the wind and the rain, so they will just romp away.

The biggest problem with conservatory gardening is controlling the heat in summer. A conservatory facing the sun during summer (that is, south-facing if you live in the northern hemisphere, and north-facing if you live in the

ABOVE **If you have the space, the financial wherewithal and of course the inclination, there is nothing to prevent you from creating your own exotic or jungle paradise within your own home conservatory.**

southern hemisphere) is the biggest culprit as, unless you can provide some form of shading, there's a very good chance that certain plants will be scorched in the heat and strong, direct sunlight. Shading for a conservatory usually comes in the form of attractive blinds that can be pulled back and forth as necessary. There are plenty of specialists who will make to order and fit your conservatory blinds for you. When done, the plant world is at your beck and call.

ABOVE **Most home conservatories these days are an extension on our indoor living spaces — but they usually form the perfect conditions for growing a wide range of tender plants.**

PLANTS TO GROW IN A CONSERVATORY

Here are just a few favourite plants for growing in a conservatory:

- Glory lily (*Gloriosa superba* 'Rothschild-iana'), an exotic-looking climber with vivid scarlet red and yellow flowers.
- Sago palm (*Cycas revoluta AGM*), this is a palm-like plant that is often sold small, but can get large, at which point it can be planted outdoors in a sheltered spot.
- Bromeliads and air plants; these are epiphytes, meaning that they can be grown on other plants (usually attractive tree bark and branches) for support only – they don't need soil.
- Cacti and succulents – which don't mind the bright light and dry conditions.
- Oriental lilies which have large, flamboyant flowers, and the bulbs of which are readily available from garden centres.
- Potted citrus trees: Meyer lemons and Calamondin oranges will just love being in a large pot in the corner of your conservatory, and they will not get much bigger than a metre high.

LEFT **Just as with other forms of 'under cover' gardening, the conservatory can overheat in sunny weather. If you have plants growing in a conservatory it is crucially important, therefore, to ensure that you open the windows and doors to provide adequate ventilation at such times.**

USING WATER UNDER COVER

Watering plants living under cover is a vital thing to get right as they will be the most demanding of regular water supply. There are a few different ways to do this, depending on what kind of structure you have.

HAND WATERING

In other words, using a watering can! The most convenient form of watering in the confined space of a greenhouse is via a watering can. Those with longer spouts are better at reaching plants at the back of staging. Water may be used either straight from the tap (preferably fitted in the greenhouse), or from a storage tank positioned under the staging.

If this is filled by rainwater from the greenhouse guttering, fit some kind of filter over the inlet to keep out leaves and other debris which may foul the water.

ABOVE **Hand watering, using a medium-sized can with a rose fitted, is the most convenient way to water a greenhouse.**

AUTOMATIC WATERING SYSTEM

If you have to be out all day and find that the time you spend in your greenhouse or polytunnel is limited, an automatic watering system may be just what you need. This may also be the ideal solution if you are going away on holiday at a crucial time when water will be needed. There are many different types of automatic watering system on the market, and a trip to your local garden centre will reveal the full range of options available to you.

The capillary bench is very effective. This used to consist of a simple bed of sand but now units are available that use fibre matting. This is laid across a tray so one end of it rests in a reservoir of water that is kept continuously topped up by a plastic tank.

The matting draws water throughout its length and into the plants standing on it. Provided that the compost in the pots is in contact with the matting, it can draw up what moisture it needs. The matting does have a tendency to become coated with green algae, but there are chemicals that can be used to prevent this. Plastic pots can be used quite effectively with capillary watering, but clay pots must be provided with a wick, instead of crocks, which can take the water straight into the compost. A strip of the matting material leading through the hole will work.

MIST PROPAGATION

Many cuttings, particularly those which are difficult to root, can be persuaded to cooperate if they are sprayed with water from time to time, and a mist propagation unit is an automated system of doing just that. The technique, which keeps the leaves and stems of the cuttings moist, maintains the humidity and speeds up rooting.

Mist propagators incorporate a sensor, which switches on the mist when required. The most common type of sensor is known as an electronic 'leaf', which is placed among the cuttings. When it dries out, it switches on the mist until its surface is moist again. Other systems work by spraying the cuttings at timed intervals, but are not as effective as they do not react to the external weather conditions – the factors that determine if the plants are going to be dry.

Mist propagators are usually constructed on an open bench over a base heated by warming cables or a heating mat. A wide range of plant types can be rooted under mist, but this method is only regarded as essential for a few, such as some of the flowering cherries (*Prunus*), and forms of pine (*Pinus*). The biggest disadvantage is the management the mist units require to ensure the electronic leaves do not become

scaled up, or the compost too wet from over-misting. If you intend to set up your own mist propagator, experiment to find the most suitable settings, and a compost mix which does not become too wet.

Cuttings rooted under mist need very careful weaning. Some sophisticated mist unit controllers have settings to wean the cuttings, reducing the misting gradually over a period of time. If only a few trays or pots are ready to wean, then the simplest solution is to gradually move them away from the mist nozzles over a period of about a week until they are in the normal greenhouse atmosphere.

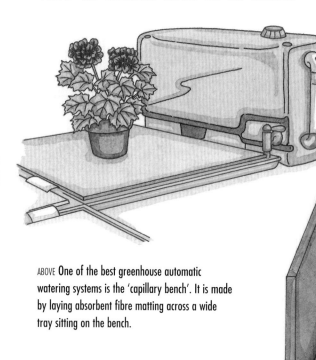

ABOVE **One of the best greenhouse automatic watering systems is the 'capillary bench'. It is made by laying absorbent fibre matting across a wide tray sitting on the bench.**

ABOVE **Mist propagation units keep the leaves of cuttings moist, reducing their water loss and speeding up the rooting process.**

ABOVE **Damping down greenhouse paths and staging during hot weather can increase humidity and make life for the plants much more bearable.**

DAMPING DOWN

One of the few instances when it is accepted practice to splash water about directly on to paving is in the greenhouse. 'Damping down' the pathways and the benches or staging helps to reduce the temperature in a greenhouse or polytunnel on very hot days, and it increases humidity (which most types of plant enjoy). The water-wise gardener should not, however, damp down indiscriminately; the practice is not necessary in winter, nor on cold, humid autumn days – in fact, it is undesirable at these times.

WATERING GARDEN FRAMES

It is a simple job to water plants in a small garden frame with a watering can or hosepipe fitted with a rose. However, this can be laborious if you have a long run of frames, such as was often the case with old-style 'estate' gardens that had to provide a constant supply of food to the 'lords of the manor'. In these situations, some system of semi-automatic watering is a great time saver and it will also be efficient in the use of the water.

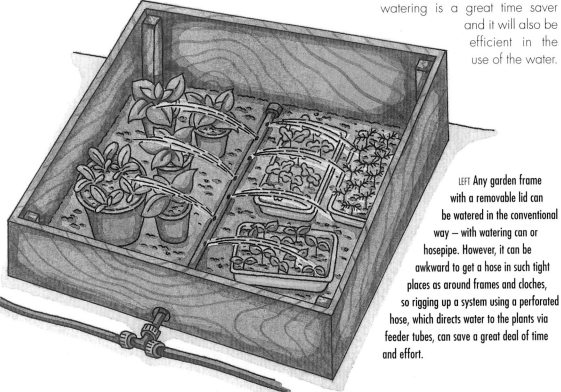

LEFT **Any garden frame with a removable lid can be watered in the conventional way – with watering can or hosepipe. However, it can be awkward to get a hose in such tight places as around frames and cloches, so rigging up a system using a perforated hose, which directs water to the plants via feeder tubes, can save a great deal of time and effort.**

WATERING UNDER CLOCHES

If you find the thought of watering a row or two of cloches rather daunting, take comfort from the fact that it will be much easier than you think and under normal weather conditions it will not be necessary very often. Through winter and spring we are usually blessed with a reasonable sprinkling of rain which seeps into the soil not only downwards but sideways as well. The largest plastic tunnel or glass cloche will be only some 2ft (60cm) wide and as both the rainwater and the plants' roots move horizontally through the soil the two will come into contact and the plants will get a drink.

There are, however, one or two things you can do to ensure the efficiency of this system. First, make sure that the soil between the cloches is well cultivated to allow water to drain through; water just runs off a hard, compacted surface. And second, keep the soil well supplied with organic matter; this helps to facilitate the quick transportation of water downwards and sideways through the soil.

During periods of dry weather you will need to water, but before rushing out with the hosepipe it is a good idea to dig a hole in the soil with a trowel to see if it is moist underneath. It may be the case that just the surface has baked in the sun, giving the impression that the soil is dry all the way down. The most susceptible plants to dryness in the top few inches of soil are seedlings and young plants with shallow root systems; these will therefore need watering sooner. Seedlings are the only plants that will need direct watering; you will need to remove the cloches and give the ground a gentle soaking with a watering can or hosepipe fitted with a fine rose.

Once plants are established, all water is applied to their roots via the soil outside the cloches. There are several ways of doing this, apart from using a watering can or hose. An oscillating or perforated hole sprinkler can be placed among the cloches and as the water runs

ABOVE **Irrigate cloches by allowing the water to run down the sides. You can even make some shallow trenches immediately next to the cloches, which will help water to penetrate the soil, rather than run off it.**

off the glass or plastic surfaces it will seep into the ground. As we have seen before, sprinklers can waste a large amount of water, so whether or not the water-wise gardener uses a sprinkler in this sort of situation will depend on the design of the area, the sorts of plants growing and whether they all need the same amount of water.

On very light soils, which drain quickly, a shallow channel taken out with a draw hoe, down each side of a row of cloches will allow the water to collect and permeate the soil closest to the plants' roots. If you possess any lengths of trickle irrigation tubing these, too, can be laid in between the rows of cloches as close to the glass as possible. A slow, steady flow of water will find its way to the plants' roots.

CHAPTER 8

Lawns and lawn care

ost gardeners enjoy being able to walk barefoot on their lawns – during summer and obviously when the weather is conducive! The grass in the Mediterranean, Middle East, Australia, even America is usually of a coarser blade, evolved (and bred) to withstand drought conditions – but it just isn't as nice to walk on. I have friends who are keen bowlers – not cricket, but crown green bowls – and whenever I see them play I spend more time admiring the fine grass and the high standard of green-keeping rather than the skills of the sports men and ladies. However, it is neither easy, nor practical, to achieve this kind of extremely fine grass effect in our own back gardens. But we do want soft, healthy lawns that are a pleasure to both look at and walk on.

ABOVE The traditional British lawn has fine, soft grasses, and is mown to show the familiar and coveted 'stripes'.

SPRINGTIME MAINTENANCE

Where your lawn is concerned spring is when you should start your yearly programme of care. My own seven point plan is as follows:

1 First cut: before mowing, lightly rake over the lawn with a wire rake to lift any grasses that have laid flat over the winter. Mow with the blades set high so that the grass is just 'topped'. Do not mow in frosty or muddy conditions.

RIGHT **The early cuts of the year should be with the mower blades set at their highest setting.**

ABOVE **Before undertaking the first cut of the year, lightly rake over the lawn with a wire rake to lift any grasses that have laid flat over the winter months.**

ABOVE **Moss, as seen here growing amongst poor, sparse grass, can grow profusely over the winter period, so it should be controlled in spring.**

2 Kill moss: apply a proprietary moss killer (or lawn sand), available from the garden centre. Most moss killers contain ferrous sulphate which will also green-up the grass. After a week or two, 'scarify' the lawn: rake it vigorously (or use an electric model) to remove the dead moss and old, rotting grass leaves, called 'thatch'.

3 Aeration: if your lawn is old, it is almost certainly compacted as well, and a way to partly counter this is to aerate it. Spike the lawn with a garden fork, penetrating the ground to at least 4in (10cm), and wiggle it around so that the holes are of a decent size. This will allow air into the soil; professionals use hollow-tined aerators that bring out a plug of soil each time, which is even more effective. There are some hand-tool hollow-tine aerators for amateurs, but for the average gardener a garden fork is a good alternative. Be thorough though, making sure that enough holes are made to make a difference.

LEFT **Aerating the lawn in its simplest form is the simple spiking of the grass using a garden fork.**

ABOVE **Special lawn spiking tools, which remove a core of soil, are available from garden centres.**

4 Carry out repairs: worn patches, damaged edges, bumps or hollows should all be tackled in spring. Where grass cover is thin, over-seed with a suitable seed mix. Straighten edges with a half-moon edging iron to create a definite edge for easier trimming later on.

5 Feeding: give the grass its first feed of the season when the grass is actively growing and the weather is warmer. Apply either a simple fertilizer, or a weed and feed brand, or even the more sophisticated weed, feed and moss killer types. But do not use a fertilizer high in nitrogen this early in the season, as it will encourage soft, lush growth that will be prone to disease. Most lawn fertilizers you can buy at the garden centre will tell you whether they are for spring, summer or autumn application.

6 Weeding: about two weeks after the feeding, spray with a selective lawn weedkiller. Feeding the lawn beforehand ensures that the weeds are growing strongly, with a larger leaf area to absorb the chemical.

7 Mowing: you should mow the grass whenever it needs it – and this applies at any time of year, but from late autumn to early spring there is usually a respectable winter break. If we have a dry summer the rate of grass growth will be slow, and you will not need to mow very often at all. If we have a wet summer, however, you could find yourself mowing twice a week.

AUTUMN MAINTENANCE

Autumn, too, is a time to take stock of what is happening to the grass and, where possible, to make corrections. Here is my six-point plan for autumn lawn care:

1 First rains: wait until the first autumn rains soften the ground, particularly if your soil is heavy clay; otherwise jobs will be difficult to carry out and you risk doing more harm than good to the lawn.

2 Collect leaves: as autumn leaves fall make sure you collect them on a regular basis – at least once a week. If you leave them, and they get wet with rain or dew, they will start to decompose in situ, compact themselves, and kill the grass underneath. In addition, they will become slippery and dangerous to walk on.

3 Feeding: Apply one of the autumn fertilizers available. These are designed to strengthen and build up the lawn in preparation for the cold

ABOVE **Brush autumn leaves off the lawn regularly, otherwise they can encourage diseases of the grass.**

winter months. They contain a mixture of nutrients, but unlike the spring and summer feeds, nitrogen (the element that encourages soft, leafy growth) is only supplied in a small amount. With proportionately more potassium and phosphorous, the fertilizer will stimulate root growth and encourage winter hardiness and disease resistance.

ABOVE **You can remove fallen leaves from the lawn by going over them with a lawn mower, but make sure it is the type that has a collecting bag, so that you can transfer them to the compost heap.**

ABOVE **Brushing the lawn occasionally to disperse autumn morning dew helps to prevent fungal diseases.**

ABOVE **Top dressing the lawn with good, soil, sand, garden compost and peat, should take place every autumn.**

4 Pest disease and moss control: Brushing the lawn occasionally to disperse autumn morning dew helps prevent fungal diseases. Look out for patches of yellow or distressed grass, especially if the autumn weather is mild and wet. Chemical control is sometimes available, but most of the minor lawn diseases are best rectified by better cultivation practices (including brushing and good, regular aeration).

A cool, damp autumn sees the return of moss and you will need to apply a mosskiller to control it. It may be best to choose an autumn fertilizer that contains ferrous sulphate. This will kill moss, and at the same time act as a lawn tonic. Once the moss has turned black, rake it out by hand or with a mechanical scarifier.

Worm casts are the small patterned, worm-like mounds of soil – the spoil created by worms as they tunnel through the soil under a lawn. Casts can be a nuisance, particularly on fine, closely mown lawns. If you leave these casts they will kill the patch of grass underneath them, and this is made worse if you walk on them and flatten them. Wait for them to dry on a fine day and sweep them off with a stiff brush.

5 Spiking and top dressing: Spiking is more important in the spring, to get air into the soil around the grass roots, to build up the condition of the plants in readiness for summer. But it has almost as much relevance in autumn, to get the lawn ready for winter, and this is especially the case if your soil is heavy clay. Spike the lawn as described for spring.

Top dressing is the application of bulky material (such as a mixture of good quality soil, sand and garden compost or peat) to the surface of the lawn. It is best carried out in autumn, as it is designed to fill in all the minor hollows which have developed during the year, and over a number of years it builds up an ideal soil layer. Spread the mixture at the approximate rate of 3lb per sq yd (1.3kg per 0.8m²), using a spade to put down small heaps over the surface. This is then brushed into the lawn so that the particles are not resting on the blades of grass, but worked down to soil level.

6 Over-seeding: Bare patches can be over-seeded with a suitable seed mixture. The seed should germinate quickly in the moist conditions of autumn, and will normally establish before the winter gets under way.

SUMMER AND WINTER MAINTENANCE

Neither at the height of summer nor during the depths of winter are times to do much with the lawn, mainly because the grass is under a certain amount of stress (in the case of summer) or dormant (in the case of winter). You could consider trying the procedures that follow, where relevant:

Summer: Mow regularly; trim edges as required; spot treat patches of weeds; feed lightly and/or apply lawn weedkiller in early summer; and water new lawns as required. In cold areas grass seed may be sown in late summer (although early autumn is generally the preferred time).

Winter: In warmer climates mowing may still be necessary; turfing may also be undertaken; clear leaves from grass areas; if rainwater is standing on the surface and not soaking away readily, consider improving the drainage of the area (major upheaval, but necessary in some instances); overhaul the mower and other lawn tools before the start of the new season.

From mid-winter onwards, check regularly for signs of worm activity and disperse worm casts. A mosskiller can be applied in late winter (if the weather is settled). Begin soil preparation if a new lawn is to be laid.

ABOVE **During the summer trim the edges of the lawn every couple of weeks; it is surprising how much better a lawn can appear if it is edged well.**

ABOVE **Spot treat weeds in summer, rather than applying an all-over selective weedkiller. Large-leaved perennial weeds, such as dandelion, should be treated this way.**

MAKING A LAWN

Whether you want to make repairs to an existing lawn, or create an entirely new lawn, spring and autumn are the ideal times to lay turf or sow grass seed. But preparation is the key to success, and although it may seem arduous to prepare properly, it must be done.

PREPARATION

Ideally, the ground should be dug, but if you lack the time or the inclination to do this then you can rotavate the whole area; this is much easier and quicker than digging. All weeds should be killed off with a weedkiller first. If you can get hold of large quantities of bulky organic matter (a bulk load of coir, peat, leafmould or mushroom compost, for example), spread it evenly over the surface of the soil and rotavate it in. After digging or rotavating you should tread the area well and rake it level roughly. Then rake in 2oz per sq yd (60g per m²) of Growmore fertilizer. After this comes the topping – turf or seed. Turf is more expensive but can be walked on after six weeks or so. Seed is cheaper, though it will be some months before it will be able to take normal foot traffic.

TURFING

Turf comes in pieces, the most common size being 3 x 1ft (90 x 30cm) and you should first lay a strip all round the edge. Then, starting on the straightest side, lay a plank on the edge and working from it put down the next row. Make sure the joints do not align – stagger and bond the turfs alternately, like bricks in a wall. When you have finished, rake in some old potting compost, sharp sand or sifted soil to fill any cracks. Then water the lawn. A sprinkler in situ for about 20 minutes will do the job of thoroughly moistening the turf, the joints and the top inch or so of soil underneath – this will be sufficient for getting the turf to bond with the soil and, provided temperatures are 45°F (7°C) or higher, the grass should grow.

ABOVE **Turf is usually supplied in rolls, but they should not be left like this for more than a day or two, otherwise the grass will start to deteriorate.**

SEEDING

If you sow seed the first thing to do is buy the right type. It comes in hard-wearing mixtures, mixtures for shady areas and mixtures for a bowling-green type finish. Garden centres sell it by the packet, which may be enough to cover, say 6–12 sq yds (5–10 m2), or more. Alternatively, if you are just wanting to sow a small amount of seed, say over a bare patch within the lawn, then there are smaller 'patch packets' available.

Grass seed is usually sown at the rate of about 1½ oz per sq yd (50g per m²). Weigh out the amount recommended on the packet, put it in an old yoghurt pot and mark the level with a felt-tipped pen. Now, using two garden lines, or a series of bamboo canes, lay out a strip divided into yards or metre squares. One fill of the pot to the marked level should then be sprinkled as evenly as you can manage into each of the marked areas. Move the string and/or canes until you have gone over the whole plot. Now rake the area well – though you will not be able to, nor should you, cover all of the seed.

Most seed these days is treated to be unpalatable, though not poisonous, to birds. At least one company is selling the seed dyed blue, because this is not a colour birds associate with food. However, birds can still have dust baths in the large area of finely raked soil, which can cause nasty holes in your germinating lawn. Cats, also, can do their business in such a place and then scuff the soil to cover their droppings. It may be wise, therefore, to stretch cotton over the area or to lay pea sticks over it.

Water the area – just as with turf, a sprinkler will probably be best, but in this case you do not want to walk over the seeded area, so a side-oscillating sprinkler rather than a rotary type is preferable. Better still, use a hand-held hosepipe, standing just outside the seeded area. Either place your thumb or finger over the end to create a fine spray to wet the seeded soil, or use a hose-end spray attachment. However you do it, the important thing is to thoroughly moisten the area, and evenly, without causing the water to run into channels which would destroy the even effect of the germinating grass.

In dry periods you will need to water the area several times, as the germinating seed (which could be in the full glare of the sun) is vulnerable to drying out. It is best to avoid watering during the heat of the day; first, because much of the water will evaporate quickly and, second because when the soil surface dries quickly in the sun it may develop a hard crust. Then, if the crust is too hard for a subsequent watering and the water does not seep through quickly, it can form into puddles.

If the soil is generally too dry for water to penetrate, use a wetting agent, such as a few drops of washing up liquid to every gallon can of water. Apply this to the ground and then activate the sprinkler or hose. Be careful not to use a detergent that contains bleach as this can damage the lawn.

When your grass grows, it is a fact of life that weeds will as well. It is at this stage you that should use a weedkiller that is specially formulated for young grass.

Cut the grass when it is about 2in (5cm) high, but just tip it; certainly do not go lower than 1in (2.5cm). Continue to cut at the same height for at least two months.

ABOVE **Start turfing a lawn by laying the first turfs on straightest side of the area, and work backwards across the lawn – never standing on the turf you have just laid.**

ABOVE **Seeding a lawn – either the whole lawn or just repairing patches – can be carried out in spring or autumn.**

WATERING ESTABLISHED LAWNS

In the 'good old days' gardeners were told to water their lawns in summer to prevent them turning to something resembling cork matting. Today's concern over water shortages means that it is neither recommended nor politically correct to water the lawn. But, I'm happy to say, this is not as disastrous as you might think. Even in the driest of summers the grass will always return to its former green state after one or two decent rainfalls. So don't panic. To help prevent the soil under your lawn from drying out too quickly, give the lawn a top dressing each autumn of bulky material as discussed on page 99. Apply at the rate of 3lb per square yard (1.3kg per 0.8m²), brushing it well in.

During dry weather never mow closely – a cutting height of 1in (2.5cm) is recommended. Mowing will be needed less often, anyway, as the growing rate of the grass will slow down. A prolonged dry period will, of course, mean that the lawn goes brown. Hopefully this will not mean that the individual grass plants actually die. If there are deep-rooted weeds present, such as dandelion, white clover and yarrow, these will remain bright green and will stand out against the beige surroundings. This will be your perfect opportunity to spot treat them with an appropriate weedkiller.

ABOVE **Watering grass is not to be recommended unless the lawn has been newly laid; using a fine mist sprinkler such as this waters the lawn in a circular pattern.**

ABOVE **An oscillating sprinkler will water the lawn in a wide, rectangular pattern, with the water jets sweeping backwards and forwards; if placed next to a flowerbed this will be watered as well.**

CHAPTER 9

The kitchen garden

ABOVE **There is nothing so satisfying as growing your own fruit and vegetables: they taste better, and you know exactly what has gone into producing them.**

In Chapter 5 we saw that it is quite possible to grow a wide range of fruits and vegetables in containers for siting on the patio, but what about an area of the garden dedicated to food crops – the kitchen garden? How can fruit and vegetables be added into a decorative garden, without making the whole garden look like a run-down allotment? And, more importantly, how does a kitchen garden fit in with our water-saving principles?

DESIGNING THE VEGETABLE PLOT

There is an important point of distinction between an ornamental garden and a kitchen garden. The latter, only accommodates plants for a relatively short period, after which the remnants are cleared, the ground dug over and fresh plants grown the following season or year. In the decorative garden you may have a tree or shrub with a life expectancy of 50 years or more. One of the quickest-maturing vegetables, the radish, can have a life-span of just six weeks.

Vegetables can be attractive plants in their own right and it is possible, within the boundaries of the ordinary domestic garden, to grow vegetables in an ornamental way.

Often the formal bed design, made up of simple geometric shapes (squares, circles, triangles and so on) is most attractive, especially in a relatively small area. Low herb hedges may be used to divide the beds, as can be found in traditional parterres and knot gardens.

It is also possible to adapt the raised bed system to provide some ornamental features: for example, the rear of the beds may be staked with decorative trelliswork. Many vegetables, such as ornamental kales or cabbages, lend themselves to the ornamental garden because of their particular shape, form or colour. However, perhaps the best way to make sure a vegetable plot 'integrates' well with the ornamental garden is to make sure that it is kept neat, tidy, edged and weed-free. It then becomes a pleasure to look at, even out of season, rather than being an eyesore.

RIGHT **Many gardeners like to grow a few decorative vegetables (here sweet peppers) in amongst their border plants in the flower garden.**

ABOVE **Vegetables can be colourful and decorative in their own right — so a vegetable garden need not look dull, green (or messy) all year round.**

WHICH VEGETABLES TO GROW

Huge encyclopaedias have been written on vegetables, and here we have just a few pages. Therefore I shall just cover the most popular types for the water-wise gardener.

SALAD PLANTS

Whatever kind of gardener you are, you cannot endure a year without growing a few salad plants. They are so easy – and so necessary for summer eating (or eating at any time). Unfortunately there is not space here to include all of the different types you could grow. Some that I would not be without, however, are rocket (hot, spicy leaves making a good substitute to lettuce), spring onions (unsurpassed for adding flavour), carrot (grated) and beetroot (whole baby beets, preferably warm, with black pepper). But if you are new to the salad game, here are the mainstay vegetables to grow:

◆ **Lettuce:** If you have an acre of vegetable garden, or just a large pot, it is possible to grow lettuce. During spring sow the seed very thinly, ½in (1cm) or so deep, either in the greenhouse or directly in the garden soil. When they are planted out, or thinned out if sown outside, they should be around 1ft (30cm) apart; or 6in (15cm) apart if you are growing the popular loose-leaf variety 'Salad Bowl'. Slugs can be a problem with lettuce, so choose your preferred control measure (bait, beer traps, or the various biological nematode controls). Always water lettuce in the morning to reduce the chance of disease.

◆ **Cucurbits:** You may not be familiar with this name, but it is the generic name for plants in the cucumber family (rather like 'Brassica' is for the cabbage family). As well as cucumbers it includes courgettes and marrows, melons, pumpkins and squashes. These can all be sown in mid-spring for planting out in early summer. Sow the large, flat seeds in 3in (8cm) pots, or large modules. Sow the seeds on edge rather than upright, as this reduces soil resistance for the seedlings. Temperature needs vary, from 13°C (55°F) for courgettes, to 25°C (77°F) for watermelons.

ABOVE **Lettuce (this is the variety 'Webb's Wonderful') is one of the most popular of salad plants.**

ABOVE **Cucumbers (this is the variety 'Telegraph') are very 'thirsty' vegetables requiring daily watering if under glass.**

◆ **Tomatoes:** These, to my way of thinking, are every bit as crucial to a salad as green leaves. But the subject of tomatoes is so huge, whole books have been written about them alone. Without the tomato (or 'love apple' to give it its old English name, in the belief that they were an aphrodisiac) about three-quarters of all savoury dishes would be missing a vital – and colourful – ingredient. It is one of our most enduring of vegetables. And yes, I maintain it IS a vegetable and not a fruit. You do not keep tomatoes in a fruit bowl, but you do eat them in savoury dishes with other vegetables. OK, technically and botanically the tomato is a 'fruit', but so are peppers, courgettes, marrows, cucumbers and all the members of the pea and bean family.

◆ **Sweet peppers and chillis:** Mid-spring is the time to sow these, in a shallow pot. Prick out the seedlings into small pots or modules of sowing compost. Keep warm at 12–25°C (54–77°F), and plant them out in early summer.

◆ **Sweet corn:** Sow in module trays or small pots at 20–27°C (68–80°F) and plant out when about 3in (8cm) tall in early summer.

ABOVE **Sweet corn can be very successful in hot summers, but you need to make sure the plants are well watered when in full growth.**

ABOVE **Tomatoes (this is 'Gardener's Delight') are easy-to-grow plants, but demand a lot of water.**

ABOVE **Sweet peppers are, like tomatoes, easy to grow but demand rather less water.**

LEGUMES

'Pod and seed' vegetables are pretty enough to be grown for their decorative qualities alone, but they are also full of vital vitamins and minerals. The vegetables can roughly be divided into those that produce edible seeds (peas and broad beans) and those that are grown for their edible pods (runner beans and mangetout peas). The pods of French or dwarf beans can be eaten, or just the seeds from within them. The range of colours among all of these legumes, not only their flowers but also of the pods, is breathtaking. And their delicate tendrils, constantly reaching out to find something to cling on to, are sweetly pretty.

ABOVE French (or dwarf) beans are not as popular with amateur gardeners, but they do produce a good yield for the effort and space they take up.

◆ **Garden peas:** When picked straight from the pod these are so sweet that they can be eaten raw as a snack. They are often described as round or wrinkled – not a precise description of the shape of the pea, but more as a way of classifying them as hardy (round for autumn sowing) or tender (wrinkled for spring sowing). Sow them straight outdoors 1–2in (2.5–5cm) deep and 2–3in (5–7cm) apart. Harvest them around 12 weeks after sowing.

◆ **Mangetout and sugar snap peas:** These are bred to be eaten whole, pod and all. Mangetout (French for 'eat all') are ready when the pods are flat, before the peas inside have developed. Sugar snaps should be eaten once the peas are fully developed and the pods have rounded out. Sow and harvest as above.

◆ **French or dwarf beans:** The taller climbing beans are especially useful for smaller gardens, as they can be grown to scramble up an arch in a flower border. They are also prolific! In fact, the more you pick them, the more they will grow. Haricot beans are the dried, mature bean seeds; flageolet beans, the tender, delicately flavoured beans so popular in France, are actually the half-ripe, shelled bean seeds. Sow outdoors in spring where they are to grow.

◆ **Runner beans:** These have been a staple in our diet for generations. This is the most ornamental of the bean family, with flowers of

ABOVE Runner beans (this is the variety 'Enorma') are popular, but they do not a lot of water.

bright red, orange or white, depending on the variety. Dwarf varieties are especially suited to exposed gardens as they are less affected by wind than the taller climbers. Planning ahead is the key to getting a good runner bean crop, as the soil should be prepared about six months beforehand (in the 'ideal world'!). Dig in masses of well-rotted compost or manure and dig deep, as runner bean roots go down a long way. Sow in individual pots in the greenhouse, or outdoors 6in (15cm) apart from the end of May. Picking should start about 12 weeks from sowing.

◆ **Broad (or fava) beans:** Hated by children (in my experience), but loved by many – including me! These are so easy to grow; they will even germinate on a piece of damp newspaper! Broad beans are very hardy, extremely prolific and top of the list as nutrition providers. Sow the beans outdoors in autumn or spring 9in (23cm) apart. Harvest them from mid-summer onwards, picking them while they are still young and tender.

There are also 'kidney' beans, and 'butter' (or Lima) beans, but these are tropical crops generating mixed results in temperate regions.

ROOT CROPS

These are the potatoes, carrots, beetroot, parsnips, turnips, swedes, the roots of which are eaten. They are perfect for the low-water garden, as they do not usually need supplementary watering (the all-important moisture-absorbing root hairs are down where the water is!).

◆ **Potatoes:** These are by far the most frequently grown. I thoroughly enjoy nipping down the garden and digging up a plant to find 20 or 30 healthy, clean tubers. They can be cooked and eaten within the hour, and the taste can be out of this world. The only downside to growing potatoes at home, I suppose, is that they can take up quite a bit of space. Doing it properly, you would need to space 'first early' varieties every 12in (30cm) or so in rows some 24in (60cm) apart, and a bit more than this for the 'second earlies' and 'maincrops'.

ABOVE **Potatoes (this is the red-skinned variety 'Red Duke of York') need plenty of water when the above-ground green growths are at their most voluminous.**

ABOVE **Broad beans are loved and hated in equal measure: they are not difficult and need a medium amount of water to survive.**

109

POTATO JARGON

In order to grow potatoes means that you must be familiar with a bit of jargon:

First early varieties: planted in early spring, for harvesting in summer

Second early varieties: planted up to mid-spring for lifting in mid-summer

Maincrop varieties: planted in late spring; lifting can take place in mid-summer for using immediately, or you can wait until early autumn for lifting and storing, which means that they can be used in the winter.

'Seed' potatoes: this does not mean seed as in 'a packet of seed'. It actually refers to a smallish potato tuber, usually the size of a hen's egg, and which has on it several healthy 'eyes' or buds, from which the shoots and roots will grow once the seed is planted. The garden centre offers bags of 'seed' potatoes that are clearly marked with the variety and type, so you can always tell when to plant and harvest them.

◆ **Carrots:** This is the next popular crop, and very easy to grow; carrots require a soil that is neither too stony nor freshly manured. Otherwise, they are not too demanding of time and expertise. Carrot root fly is the only problem a gardener growing them is likely to come across; unfortunately there are no chemicals to control this fly, so if your crop is susceptible it is recommended to put up a barrier around the plants, some 2ft (60cm) high, as the flies do not generally fly above this height.

THE ONION FAMILY

This is very large, for not only does it include many different types of onion (salad, pickling, red and white varieties of many different sizes), it also has in it chives, shallots, garlic and leeks.

In all cases you can sow seeds, but for shallots you usually plant the small bulbs, which multiply over the growing season, and for garlic you plant a segment of the bulb (known as a clove). Leeks comprise a long stem-like collection of rolled leaves, unlike any other vegetable and, it has to be said, not much like onions either. These are not difficult, but are different in their growing as when planting you just drop the young leek plant into a hole made by a dibber, and trickle in some water. There is no firming or packing soil around the roots to be done.

ABOVE **Being deep-rooted, carrots (these are 'Chantenay Red Cored') do not need so much water supplied.**

ABOVE There are many different and varied members of the onion family – including leeks, garlic, chives and shallots – but the most popular types are always the round-bulbed varieties of onion used raw and in cooking.

THE CABBAGE FAMILY

Equally as large as the onion family, the brassicas include such luminaries as cabbage (spring, summer, autumn and winter varieties), cauliflower, broccoli and calabrese, Brussels sprouts, kale, turnips and swedes. Being root crops, and therefore very different in habit and shape to their 'green' cousins, the last two are not usually thought of as brassicas. But they are, and just as susceptible to all of the foibles and weaknesses of the main members of the family – such as vulnerability to the fungal disease clubroot, and prone to attack by birds. Brassicas are very valuable additions to any kitchen garden, however, and they also have the benefit of not being particularly thirsty vegetables.

ABOVE Cabbages are the most widely grown member of the brassica family, which also includes broccoli, cauliflower, kale, Brussels sprouts, turnips and swedes.

THE FRUIT GARDEN

Mid-autumn is the principal time for planting fruit trees – allowing them to get their roots established in the ground before winter sets in. But which fruits should you choose? The answer is two-fold. First, it depends on how much space you have and, second, what you like.

TREE FRUITS

If you have the space, and you enjoy eating them, the tree fruits can give enjoyment in both the growing and the eating.

◆ **Apples:** The apple is singularly the most popular fruit, which is most fortunate as they grow very well in temperate climates. Dessert varieties are always to be preferred over the cooking (or 'culinary') apples, as the former can be picked and eaten straight off the tree. They can be grown in compact, trained form, such as cordons or espaliers, so even a small garden can have a couple of varieties. Choose self-pollinating types such as 'Falstaff', 'Greensleeves', 'Herefordshire Russet' or 'Queens Cox'. The garden centre will also

ABOVE **Pears are not as popular as apples – to both grow and eat – but they are good for anyone with a sweet tooth.**

stock plenty of other varieties for you to choose from. In order to choose a cooking apple, such as 'Arthur Turner', 'Lord Derby' or, of course, 'Bramley's Seedling', you should be into pies, crumbles and chutney in a big way!

◆ **Pears:** Delicious and sweet (and they go really well with chocolate!). Try 'Concorde', 'Onward' or 'Williams' Bon Chretien'.

◆ **Peaches, nectarines and apricots:** You will not achieve the heaviest of yields for the amount of space you give over to them, but my goodness, the exotic flavour of these fruits when picked fresh off the tree has to be experienced to be believed. Look for peach 'Rochester', nectarine 'Lord Napier' and apricot 'Moorpark'.

◆ **Plums:** Small trees are available these days (using a type of dwarfing root system called St Julien 'A'). Look for 'Czar', 'Victoria' (the most popular of all), or the delicious, bright yellow 'Oullins Golden Gage'.

ABOVE **Apples (this is the variety 'Merton Worcester') are perfect for small gardens: they are decorative trees and produce excellent crops. But they need watering well in their formative years.**

ABOVE **Dessert cherries (this is the variety 'Stella') have a short-lived fruiting season – but they are delicious, and decorative.**

- ◆ **Sweet cherries:** These have a short-lived fruiting season, but the fruits are delicious and decorative in summer. There's an added bonus of lovely spring cherry blossom as well. Try 'Stella' or 'Morello'.

- ◆ **Nuts:** Brazil nuts, pistachios and peanuts (the latter are not technically nuts anyway, as they grow under the ground) need hot climates to grow, but hazels and walnuts can be grown in abundance! Hazel (or cob) nuts and filberts are closely related. They are both small trees, bearing separate male and female flowers on the same tree. The male flowers are the familiar catkins and the female flowers are small, red and unobtrusive. These trees are wind pollinated, and two varieties are needed to ensure good cross-pollination; ideally they should be planted next to one another, about 4.5m (15ft) apart, to help this process. The best variety to go for is 'Cosford'.

  Walnuts are difficult to find, but are fun to try. A first nut crop will occur three or four years after planting – it used to be 20 years or so, but breeding has reduced the bearing age. Look for the varieties 'Broadview', 'Buccaneer' or 'Metcalfe', which are considered by many to be the best.

SOFT FRUITS

I find myself drawn to a row of ripening raspberry canes and I can never eat just one… I do not know what it is about raspberries. Of course, I love strawberries too, and there are few sensations better than a juicy, sweet strawberry ripped straight off the plant. But raspberries, for me, are superior in taste. They can be sharper (a lot sharper!) than a strawberry, but they can also be juicier and sweeter. But it's not just raspberries that do it for me. All of the cane fruits are quite delicious. These are the blackberries, loganberries and tayberries. Autumn is the best time to plant them: the soil is still warm from summer, so plants will get established fairly quickly, and they will then romp away in the spring. If you wait until spring before you plant them, the soil will be colder and it will take them much longer to become established. So, what is what in the world of berried treasures?

- ◆ **Raspberry:** There are actually two types – those that fruit in the summer, and those that are ready in the autumn and even into early winter. The summer varieties have quite a short

ABOVE **Raspberries (this is the autumn-fruiting variety 'Autumn Bliss') are often regarded as tasting better than strawberries – which are many times more popular.**

ABOVE Blackberries (this is the variety 'Oregon Thornless', preferred by many because it does not possess vicious thorns) are vigorous but highly productive plants.

season; however they do produce high yields. The autumn types on the other hand will bear fruits from the end of summer through to the first frosts. Raspberries will not like a light, dry soil. Instead, for best results, they need a really moisture-retentive soil packed full of goodness, from well-rotted manure to garden compost.

◆ Blackberries: These are generally dismissed as, at worst, a nuisance to be eliminated, and at best as wild berries – fun to pick from hedgerows, yet not worth growing. However, if you grow some in your garden, with a little bit of feeding and weeding, and considered watering in summer, you will harvest a more bountiful crop than wild berries ever produce. These fruits are extremely hardy, and are untroubled by spring frosts and all but the driest of soils. They do, however, spread and so need a great deal of space. They are generally sold as one-year-old canes; choose thornless varieties if possible as they are slightly less vigorous and much, much easier to pick!

◆ Hybrid berries: These have raspberry and blackberry in their parentage, and the first hybrid cross took place in the late 1700s, in California; it resulted in the loganberry. The tayberry followed shortly afterwards, and now there are various others, including the sunberry and dewberry. They all combine the size and juiciness of blackberries with the sweetness of raspberries (in my view tayberries being the slightly sweeter). They freeze especially well, losing none of their flavour, and staying firm. Allow at least one season after planting before reaping a crop – this delay is more than made up for by the fact that the canes will carry on being productive for many years.

◆ Strawberries: These give the quickest return of all fruits, and can even carry a crop in their first year (although it is not advisable, as it is a good idea to build up the plant's strength by removing flowers in the first summer after planting). There are three distinct kinds of strawberry – the summer fruiting, the perpetual (or remontant) and the alpine strawberries. They all prefer a warm, sunny, sheltered position; this kind of position usually guarantees the best-flavoured berries.

ABOVE Strawberries are the favourite of many kitchen gardeners – but they do need watering well during dry weather. This is the variety 'Aromel'.

THE KITCHEN AND FRUIT GARDEN IN A DROUGHT

It is important to be able to identify signs of a vegetable in need of water. The first indications are usually quite subtle: leaves that are usually lustrous start to appear dusty and dull; stems and foliage feel less resilient when handled, and the normal rate of growth seems to have slowed down. Serious symptoms, from which plants may not recover completely, include flagging and discoloured leaves and limp stems, haphazard flowering with little or no setting, and the swelling of fruits and pods seems to stop. For anyone concerned about growing vegetables in dry conditions (such as those demonstrated by a dry, sandy soil, or perhaps you live in a low-rainfall area), there are a number of factors that can help you succeed.

ABOVE **Fruit trees (this is the apple 'Golden Delicious') need an open site in full sun.**

THE LOCATION

Most vegetables and soft fruit will only grow well in a light, open, sunny site that is well sheltered from the wind. Top or tree fruits are hardier, but they will not appreciate a garden that is too exposed. If you do have a very exposed garden, some form of windbreak should be provided that filters the air but does not cast shade. If drainage is poor, it may be improved by adding grit or sharp sand.

ABOVE **The best way to reduce the effects of a summer drought on a kitchen garden is to dig in plenty of organic matter during the previous autumn and winter.**

THE SOIL

The usual advice to dig and incorporate plenty of bulky organic matter almost goes without saying (this was discussed in Chapter 3). However, it is important not to dig or walk on the soil when it is wet as this will lead to compaction and a lack of oxygen in the soil.

THE BED

To get round this problem it is becoming more common to develop a 'bed system' comprising beds that are each no more than 5ft (1.5m) wide. This means that they can be worked from both sides without having to walk on the soil. This technique regularly produces a higher yield (per area) than conventional vegetable gardens; it reduces heavy digging and the need for weeding, and is ideally suited to laying down pipes for automatic irrigation.

THE RAISED BED

It is also possible to adapt the bed system. Raising the beds to about 18in (45cm) above adjacent ground, using old railway sleepers, building blocks or even old planks of wood, makes maintenance easy, and is particularly recommended if the gardener is infirm in some way. Raised beds, or deep beds as they are sometimes called, are ideal for gardens that have poor, shallow or badly drained soil.

THE WATERING

Just like more than 99 per cent of all members of the plant kingdom, vegetables take up water though their roots and so it is preferable to provide whatever water is necessary at root level and not onto either the green parts of the plants, or the surface of the soil. You can use a drip or trickle irrigation system as described in Chapter 4. These, arguably, were originally conceived for placing between rows of vegetables, and if you choose to use one it has the advantage of being easy to move wherever it is needed.

Water the vegetable plot no more than twice weekly, but when you do, make sure the soil around the roots of the plants is thoroughly soaked. This is far more important than a daily splash-about, where little water actually penetrates the soil.

Where raised or deep beds are used, the watering system can be built into the initial construction, with flexible hoses that can be placed next to the roots of plants requiring water. With regard to watering fruit plants, always water in at planting time, and check regularly for dryness for the first year, watering as appropriate. In the case of bush fruits (blackcurrant, redcurrant, whitecurrant and gooseberry) it is normally advised to apply water at around 4½ gallons per sq yd (20 litres per m²) every ten days during dry periods from flowering until harvest time. The effectiveness of this will vary depending on the temperatures endured and the condition of the soil, but it is a good guide. In the case of cane fruits keep the water off the canes as much as possible, to minimize fungal problems.

ABOVE These days gardeners are increasingly dividing kitchen gardens into smaller beds, to reduce the amount of walking on the soil, which aids the soil structure and water retention.

WATERING REQUIREMENTS FOR VEGETABLES

If one is aware of the watering requirements of the vegetables one is growing it is possible, by growing those with the same requirements together, to save wasting large quantities of water. For example, I have grouped certain vegetables here by their water requirements:

◆ **High water use:** Vegetables requiring constant watering during dry weather include runner beans, celery, calabrese, lettuce, spinach, early potatoes, courgettes, marrow and tomatoes.

◆ **Medium water use:** Vegetables requiring watering at key stages in their growth include French and broad beans, peas, summer cabbage, cauliflower, maincrop potato and sweet corn.

◆ **Low water use:** Vegetables requiring very little or no water include beetroot, broccoli, Brussels sprouts, spring cabbage, winter cabbage, winter cauliflower, carrots, parsnips, turnips, leeks and onions.

ABOVE ...Brussels sprouts...

ABOVE Low-water vegetables include broccoli and calabrese...

ABOVE ...carrots...

ABOVE **...onions...**

ABOVE **...turnips...**

ABOVE **...and winter cauliflower...**

ABOVE **...winter cabbages**

SECTION TWO

LEFT **Osteospermums are sun-loving perennials from South Africa — and perfect for the low-water garden.**

TYPICAL PLANT HARDINESS ZONES FOR WESTERN EUROPE

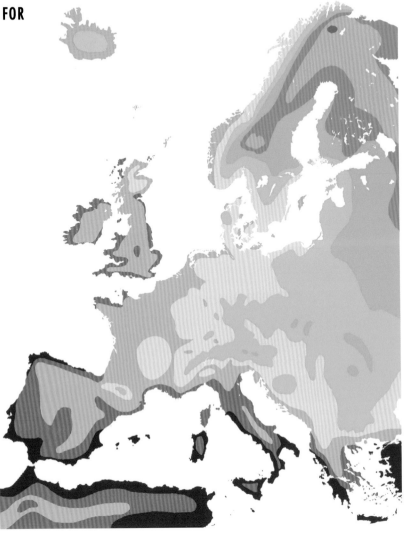

When one talks of plants with a low water requirement one immediately thinks of plants that grow in the sunniest and/or hottest countries. This is not always the case. There are many plants, including evergreen shrubs, trees and climbers, that require a dryish soil, without necessarily the warmer temperatures and long sunshine hours. It is worth remembering, also, that new plants are being developed all the time and often it is hardiness, and other weather tolerances, that is being bred into them.

Therefore it is useful to know, when buying your plants, which climate suits them best – the parts of the world in which they originate usually dictate this. If you live in Europe or the US, the maps on these pages will give you an indication of the plant hardiness zones for where you live. And as you will see from the directory section that follows, plants for dry soils can be adaptable, so wherever you live you should be able to find a selection of good plants that suit you and your garden's requirements.

TYPICAL PLANT HARDINESS ZONES FOR NORTH AMERICA

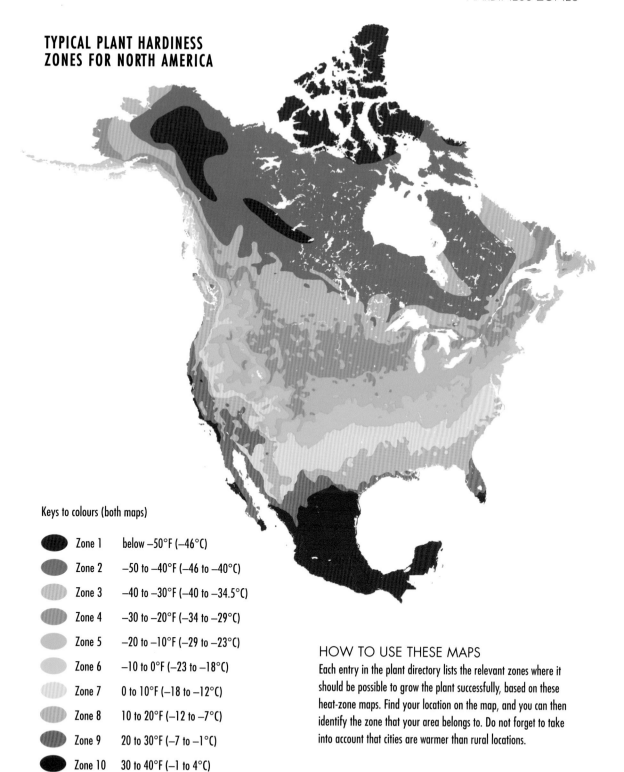

Keys to colours (both maps)

●	Zone 1	below −50°F (−46°C)
●	Zone 2	−50 to −40°F (−46 to −40°C)
●	Zone 3	−40 to −30°F (−40 to −34.5°C)
●	Zone 4	−30 to −20°F (−34 to −29°C)
●	Zone 5	−20 to −10°F (−29 to −23°C)
●	Zone 6	−10 to 0°F (−23 to −18°C)
●	Zone 7	0 to 10°F (−18 to −12°C)
●	Zone 8	10 to 20°F (−12 to −7°C)
●	Zone 9	20 to 30°F (−7 to −1°C)
●	Zone 10	30 to 40°F (−1 to 4°C)
●	Zone 11	above 40°F (above 4°C)

HOW TO USE THESE MAPS

Each entry in the plant directory lists the relevant zones where it should be possible to grow the plant successfully, based on these heat-zone maps. Find your location on the map, and you can then identify the zone that your area belongs to. Do not forget to take into account that cities are warmer than rural locations.

CHAPTER 10

A–Z directory of low-water plants

This part of the book will be an invaluable source of reference when you come to choose plants that have a low water requirement. Listed here are many of our most popular garden plants for dry situations; they are listed alphabetically within the section that relates to their type (annuals, bulbs, perennials, trees, shrubs and so on). Under each of the descriptions are these items of information:

Origin: This tells you, if known, where the species was discovered. Understanding where a plant comes from: the country or part of the world, with it average climate or even altitude, can help you to understand its growing requirements and conditions.

Type: The 'type' of plant – for example, whether it is grown from a bulb as opposed to a tuber, corm or rhizome, or whether it is an annual (grows, flowers and dies within one year) or a biennial (the same but in two years), or perhaps a shrub rather than a climber.

USDA zone: These are the climate zones referred to on pages 122 and 123, designed to identify the relative hardiness of plants. The zone numbers quoted here, based on UK Royal Horticultural Society data, are on the cautious side, so if you are not prepared to take any chances, follow the hardiness ratings to the letter. Otherwise there is a great deal of leeway. Raised beds, good drainage, tree cover, east-facing as opposed to west-facing gardens, and planting against a house wall all give plants a better habitat – so be prepared to experiment.

Description: Here you will discover generalized details of the plant's shape, size and general demeanour, along with flower and foliage colour and shape.

Popular species and varieties: Sometimes a plant species will exist without offspring or siblings. This will therefore have a relatively small entry in this book. But with, for example, the *Papaver* (poppy) genus, there are dozens of different species and cultivars (abbreviation of 'cultivated variety'), and so there will be many to recommend.

ANNUALS AND BIENNIALS

ABOVE *Antirrhinum* 'Pearly Queen Mixed'

ABOVE *Begonia semperflorens* 'President Mixed'

NAME: *ANTIRRHINUM MAJUS* (SNAPDRAGON)

Origin: Man-made hybrids from parent plants originating throughout the temperate parts of the world

Type: Tender perennial grown as an annual

USDA Zone: Z7

Description: This is arguably one of the most recognizable of bedding plants. Its flowers open like a mouth when they are squeezed gently. Plants that are not removed from the garden in autumn will usually survive in winter (provided it is not too harsh), and they will flower again for a second year; the best flowers, however, are always on young, or first-year plants. Tall-growing varieties can be used as cut flowers in the home. Dwarf types are best used as main bedding or edging plants.

Popular species and varieties: Seed catalogues usually carry a wide selection of snapdragons, ranging in height from 6–36in (15–90cm). Trailing types, such as 'Luminaire' and 'Pearly Queen Mixed', are good for using in hanging baskets and containers. 'Dancing Flame' has predominantly orange flowers but with attractive variegated foliage.

NAME: *BEGONIA SEMPERFLORENS* (BEDDING OR WAX BEGONIA)

Origin: South America

Type: Tender perennial grown as an annual

USDA Zone: Z9–11

Description: Some types of *Begonia* have bulb-like tuberous roots, but all of the bedding begonias are fibrous-rooted. These are in the 8–12in (20–30cm) height range, and possess bronze to green leaves. Flowers of white, pink or red, up to 1in (2.5cm) across, bloom continuously outdoors in summer. Many varieties with single or double blossoms, some quite large, whilst others have numerous clusters of small flowers.

Popular species and varieties: Look for the 'politicians' series: Ambassador Series, Senator Series and President Series – all are particularly good bedders. 'Stara Mixed' have large flowers, and 'Two Tones' comprises a mixture of bicolours each with dark bronze and green foliage – the 'two tone' effect. The cultivar 'Gin' has attractive bronze leaves and white flowers with yellow stamens.

NAME: *CELOSIA ARGENTEA* (COCKSCOMB)

Origin: Tropical and sub-tropical Asia, Africa and America
Type: Hardy annual
USDA Zone: Z9
Description: These plants are used in bedding schemes when planted en masse, or they make fine specimen pot plants for a greenhouse or conservatory. The flowers come in dense plumes, giving rise to an alternative common name of Prince of Wales' Feathers.

Popular species and varieties: *Celosia argentea* is divided into two groups: the Plumosa types are best for bedding out, and the Cristata types that have crested flowers and make better pot plants (if this latter type are bedded out and the summer is wet, water can rest in the flattened flowerheads, causing them to rot). The Plumosa Century Series, of which 'Century Fire' is one of the most vibrant-coloured forms, is the best for bedding. *C. spicata* has slender flower spikes and can also be used as cut flowers; to my mind the best form being 'Flamingo Feather' with pinkish flowers.

ABOVE *Celosia* 'Century Fire'

NAME: *COREOPSIS* (TICKSEED)

Origin: North and South America
Type: Tender perennial mainly grown as an annual
USDA Zone: Z4–5
Description: There are several varieties, all of which are notable for their bright daisy flowers. To some they are vulgar, but it is largely a matter of placing. All are good for cutting and bringing indoors. These are free-flowering plants and are good for the sunny border.

Popular species and varieties: Forms of *Coreopsis tinctoria*, of which 'Mahogany Midget' is one of the deepest coloured, bloom throughout summer and early autumn. *C. verticillata* is extremely floriferous and may be found in shades of yellow; it grows to around 2ft (60cm). The cultivar 'Zagreb' AGM is a very uniform golden yellow. *C. grandiflora* 'Mayfield Giant' and *C. rosea* 'Sunburst' are tall varieties, up to 3ft (90cm); 'Goldfink' is only about 1ft (30cm) and longer flowering.

NAME: *ERYSIMUM CHEIRI* (WALLFLOWER)

Origin: Southern Europe
Type: Perennial sub-shrub usually grown as a hardy biennial
USDA Zone: Z7
Description: Grown for spring bedding together with tulips and other spring plants, wallflowers also make good pot plants for a cold or slightly heated greenhouse or conservatory. For best effect, space the plants 8–12in (20–30cm apart). Half the time you will find wallflowers sold under the name *Erysimum cheiri* (the correct modern name), and the rest of the time you will see it as *Cheiranthus cheiri* (the old name that should now be abandoned).

Popular species and varieties: Mostly sold in mixtures, including 'Persian Carpet Mixed' (containing many of the reds, yellows and oranges that are traditionally seen used in Persian carpets), and 'Treasure F1 Mixed' (a modern, vigorous, branching, early-flowering

ABOVE *Coreopsis* 'Mahogany Midget'

ABOVE *Erysimum cheiri* 'Mayflower'

variety). Of the single colours available, look for 'Fire King' (rich scarlet), 'Cloth of Gold' (yellow), 'Blood Red' (magenta) and 'Mayflower' (cream-yellow). The Siberian wallflower (*Erysimum x allionii*) reaches a height of 12in (30cm) and is very much like the bedding wallflower, but should be sown somewhat later, say mid-summer. Flowers are either golden or orange, otherwise the same.

NAME: *ESCHSCHOLZIA CALIFORNICA* AGM (CALIFORNIAN POPPY)

Origin: California to Oregon
Type: Hardy annual
USDA Zone: Z6
Description: This is the state flower of California, and flowers throughout summer. The silky-textured, poppy-like blooms look attractive among annuals, perennials and in rock gardens. Sow seed in its flowering position in spring and thin out seedlings to 12in (30cm) apart. It can also be sown in autumn in milder climates for earlier flowering the following year. Available in mixtures or separate colours.

ABOVE *Eschscholzia californica* 'Golden Values'

Popular species and varieties: 'Golden Values' is a lovely, warm yellow with rich, golden orange centres; 'Ivory Castle' has creamy-white flowers with pretty yellow stamens and feathery foliage; 'Rose Chiffon' has silky, double blooms of pinky rose with contrasting golden yellow centres; and 'Milkmaid' has deep cream, fluted blooms above ferny blue-green foliage.

127

NAME: *GAILLARDIA PULCHELLA* (BLANKET FLOWER)

Origin: Mexico, Southern US
Type: Half-hardy annual
USDA Zone: Z8
Description: The common name of blanket flower arises from the bright reds and yellows of the blooms, colours that are reminiscent of Native American blanket weavings, made in parts of the Americas where these plants grow wild. *Gaillardia* flowers from mid-summer to autumn. It is attractive for cutting and filling up empty spaces in the flower border. Sow seed in heat in spring and plant out 12in. (30cm) apart after frosts have finished: or sow outside later.
Popular species and varieties: 'Burgundy' is a strong, upright plant with large, flat-faced burgundy-red flowers. 'Sundance' has large, double flowers that are almost ball-shaped, coming in deep red with small, different coloured markings on the petals (and there are occasional yellow blooms). 'Goblin', also known as 'Kobold', is very floriferous, dwarf and compact with stunning daisy-like blooms; each rich red petal is tipped with gold.

NAME: *LUNARIA ANNUA* (HONESTY)

Origin: Southern Europe
Type: Biennial
USDA Zone: Z6–8
Description: The bright purple or white summer flowers of this familiar biennial are followed by the characteristic round, flattened, parchment-like seedpods. It is chiefly grown for the pods, which are excellent in dried arrangements. This fragrant, if somewhat weedy plant, enjoys dappled to light shade, and if you live in a hot part of the world the deeper the shade is the better it will grow.
Popular species and varieties: Seed of the straight species (with pink flowers), or its several named forms, is surprisingly difficult to find; however, it is worth the search. 'Alba' has white flowers, and there is also a form ('Variegata') with variegated leaves, and another with purplish foliage.

ABOVE *Gaillardia* 'Goblin' (also known as 'Kobold')

ABOVE *Lunaria annua* 'Variegata'

ABOVE *Mesembryanthemum bellidiformis* 'Livingstone Daisy'

NAME: *MESEMBRYANTHEMUM BELLIDIFORMIS* (LIVINGSTONE DAISY)

Origin: Man-made hybrids from parent plants originating in South Africa, particularly the Cape Peninsula

Type: Half-hardy annual

USDA Zone: Z9

Description: This plant flowers profusely in sunny weather and comes in many glistening colours. Ideal for rock gardens and for the front of a flowerbed. Buy young plants in spring and set them out when frosts have finished, or sow in heat in spring and plant outside after frosts. Space them 12in (30cm) apart. Can also be sown outside in late spring.

Popular species and varieties: The common name has also become a varietal name: *M. bellidiformis* 'Livingstone Daisy' produces a brilliant array of pinks, whites, magentas, oranges and creams which open with the sun. 'Lunette' has lemon-yellow flowers with a deep orange-red centre.

NAME: *NIGELLA DAMASCENA* (LOVE-IN-A-MIST)

Origin: Southern Europe and Northern Africa

Type: Hardy annual

USDA Zone: Z7

Description: This annual blooms from early summer to autumn. It thrives in a well-drained soil

ABOVE *Nigella damascena* 'Miss Jekyll'

in a sunny spot. Can be used among other annuals and in beds for cutting. The characteristic seedheads are very attractive. It self-sows readily in reasonably mild areas.

Popular species and varieties: The variety 'Dark Blue' could not be more descriptive of the colour! 'Oxford Blue' is similar, but slightly darker. 'Miss Jekyll' is a bright blue, whilst 'Persian Jewels' is a mix of blues, pinks and white. *N. papillosa* 'African Bride' has large, snowy-white blooms with the deepest black centres, whilst 'Midnight' is rich, dark purple.

ABOVE *Petunia* 'Purple Vein' (Surfinia Series)

NAME: *PETUNIA*

Origin: Man-made hybrids from parent plants originating in tropical South America
Type: Half-hardy annual
USDA Zone: Z7
Description: The familiar trumpet-shaped flowers of the *Petunia* are seen in summer gardens everywhere; and they bloom right until the autumn frosts arrive. Petunias thrive best in sunshine, but can tolerate a little dappled shade for a small part of the day. These are one of the best plants for windowboxes and other plant containers, but can also be used among other summer-flowering plants in beds and borders. Some forms are highly scented. The perennial nature of petunias has led to the development of new forms, including the Surfinia Series and Million Bells Series (the latter now properly known as *Calibrachoa*).
Popular species and varieties: The Grandiflora types are available in frilly doubles and dramatic trumpet blooms up to 5in (13cm) across. The Multiflora types have single and double flowers up to 3in (8cm) across, and with excellent weather tolerance. The Surfinia Series offers flowers named by colour; from 'Pink' and 'Magenta' through to 'Purple' and 'White'. One of the most frequently seen is the highly scented 'Blue Vein' (pale blue petals with deep purple-blue veining).

NAME: *PORTULACA* (SUN PLANT, or ROSE MOSS)

Origin: Worldwide, from warm and tropical regions
Type: Half-hardy annual
USDA Zone: Z9
Description: With a creeping, carpeting growth habit, the stems of this plant reach no higher than 6in (15cm). It flowers throughout summer. It needs a dry and very sunny position (flowers will not open unless they receive direct sunlight). It looks very attractive in a rock garden or between the stones of a paved garden. Sow where the plants are to flower, as the seedlings do not transplant well.

ABOVE *Portulaca grandiflora* 'Sundial Mixed'

Popular species and varieties: African marigold cultivars range from 8–20in (20–50cm) in height, with flowerheads up to 4in (10cm) across. The cultivars are all double-flowered. Dwarf cultivars are often top heavy, needing a spacious setting if they are not to look incongruous. Shades of yellow, cream and orange. 'Vanilla' has attractive, cream-coloured flowers. In French marigolds, red and mahogany shades are common. Cultivars range from 6–12in (15–30cm) in height, with flowerheads up to 2½in (6cm) across. Many cultivars are in shades of red and mahogany, most commonly in bi-colour combinations with yellow. 'Queen Sophia' has red flowers becoming bronze with maturity, each petal edged with gold. The Espana and Bonanza Series are both noted for their earliness and uniformity. The Afro-French marigolds are hybrids between *T. erecta* and *T. patula*.

Popular species and varieties: *Portulaca grandiflora* is the main species, and this has given rise over the years to a number of hybrids and colour strains. Some of the best include the Calypso, Cloudbeater, Magic Carpet, Sundial and Sunny Boy hybrids. A huge array of bright colours and both double and single blooms are included within these ranges.

NAME: *TAGETES* (MARIGOLD)

Origin: Man-made hybrids from parent plants originating in tropical Mexico and Central America
Type: Half hardy annual
USDA Zone: Z9
Description: There are French (*Tagetes patula*) and African marigolds (*T. erecta*) but none of them are native to France or Africa, but come originally from Central America. The leaves are dark green, and have toothed margins. They are attractive, but have a pungent aroma, which is frequently disliked.

ABOVE *Tagetes patula* 'Espana Mixed'

BULBS

NAME: *CROCUS*

Origin: Mid and Southern Europe, Middle East, Central Asia and Northern Africa

Type: Perennial corm

USDA Zone: Z4–8

Description: The *Crocus* is one of the true harbingers of spring, and is among the best known and most popular of all the early blooming bulbous plants. Most forms are easy to grow, free-flowering and increase well in suitable conditions. Despite flowering early, weak sunshine in mild weather will encourage them to open their flowers wide, making a splendid show, particularly when naturalized. They die back quickly after flowering so it is not usually necessary to restrict grass cutting.

Popular species and varieties: Dutch crocus are the most widely grown of all. Look out for the pure white 'Jeanne d'Arc', the rich purple-violet 'Queen of the Blues', the silvery lilac-blue 'Vanguard', and 'Pickwick' with its striking purple striped blooms. *Crocus tommasinianus* AGM is one of the first to flower, in late winter and early spring. Its soft lavender flowers are small and slender. There are a number of varieties. Look for: 'Whitwell Purple' (purplish-blue) and 'Ruby Giant' (deep purple). Crocus in the Chrysanthus group are free-flowering. Growing to around 3in (7.5cm) in height, they are at their best from late winter to early spring depending on conditions. Highly recommended cultivars include 'Cream Beauty' AGM (a lovely soft cream-yellow), 'Snow Bunting' AGM (white), 'Blue Pearl' AGM (a lovely delicate blue with a bronze base and silvery blue on the outside of the petals), 'Ladykiller' AGM (glistening white slender blooms, its outer petals are a rich purple edged with white), and 'E.P. Bowles' (clear yellow flowers, feathered with purple on the outside).

ABOVE *Crocus* 'Pickwick'

ABOVE *Gladiolus* 'Attraction'

ABOVE *Muscari armeniacum*

NAME: *GLADIOLUS* (SWORD LILY)

Origin: Africa (mainly South Africa), Madagascar, Arabia, Europe, Western Asia

Type: Perennial corm

USDA Zone: Z9

Description: Modern *Gladiolus* hybrids are extremely popular – but they are not hardy, so lifting the corms in the autumn and replanting in the spring is essential. Many gardeners prefer to grow them in rows in the kitchen garden, or on a spare piece of ground, to provide cut flowers for indoors. It can be difficult to find a suitable place to grow them, and they do require staking. Grow in a sunny place in good, humus-rich, well-drained soil.

Popular species and varieties: The large-flowered hybrids come in a wide range of colours with countless varieties available. Among them are: 'Advance', a glowing red, 'Jacksonville' a deep yellow with a red throat, and 'Mysterious', a ruffled rose-pink with white a centre. There are many more. Butterfly gladiolus

are smaller flowered, growing up to 36in (90cm), and are widely used in floral arrangements. The flowers of Primulinus gladioli are funnel-shaped; the upper petal forms a hood, and the florets are not so densely packed on the stem. The old cultivar 'Columbine' is still one of the best carmine-reds, 'Anitra' is a rich red and 'Lady Godiva' is white.

NAME: *MUSCARI* (GRAPE HYACINTH)

Origin: South-east Europe and Western Asia

Type: Hardy bulbous perennial

USDA Zone: Z3–8

Description: Some of the best known of spring flowers, and certainly the best-known blue ones. These are generally low, ground-hugging bulbs, and the flower spikes are usually formed as bright blue bunches, not unlike miniature up-turned grape bunches.

Popular species and varieties: *Muscari armeniacum* AGM is the most widely grown type. The leaves spread and separate as the flower spike develops; it reaches a height of 8in (20cm) and has mid-blue bell-shaped, tightly packed flowers. Look also for *M. botryoides* 'Album', a neat and compact plant with pure white, fragrant flowers. *M. latifolium* produces lower blooms of deep violet, whilst those nearer the top of the spike are mid-blue and smaller.

133

NAME: *NERINE*

Origin: South Africa
Type: Bulbous perennial
USDA Zone: Z8–9
Description: Whether you pronounce the name ne-reen, ne-rhine or ne-ry-nee, the truth is that you cannot fail to be impressed by the flowers. Several species are half hardy, which means that they will need protection from cold in winter, but one exception is *Nerine bowdenii* AGM.

ABOVE *Nerine bowdenii* **AGM**

This can be grown in a sheltered spot, ideally at the foot of a sunny wall, and adds valuable colour to the autumn garden. All other nerines are best grown as pot plants, and brought under cover for winter.

Popular species and varieties: The long-lasting bright pink flowerheads of *Nerine bowdenii* AGM appear before the foliage. Each 18–24in (45–60cm) long stem carries up to 12 blooms with undulating petals. They can be left undisturbed for several years. The Guernsey lily, *N. sarniensis*, produces bright scarlet flowers on 18in (45cm) stems. Due to its vibrant colouring it has been used to produce some of the excellent hybrids available.

NAME: *TULIPA* (TULIP)

Origin: Turkey, Central Asia
Type: Bulbous perennial
USDA Zone: Z5–8
Description: Tulips come in a huge array of colours, shapes and sizes and are indispensable for brilliant displays. They are best planted in groups in beds or borders; they are also excellent for growing in tubs and patio containers. The position chosen should be sunny, with some protection from the wind. Heights vary, with some of the species no more than 4in (10cm) high; the stately Darwin hybrids and more graceful lily-flowered types are as high as 24in (60cm). Also there are the flamboyant Parrot types, distinctive fringed types, multi-flowered types and the rather mysterious Viridifloras, their blooms having varying amounts of green in them.

Popular species and varieties: Of all the species *Tulipa tarda* AGM is one of the most desirable, its white flowers having a bright yellow base. It grows to just 4in (10cm). Slightly later flowering is *T. hageri*, its distinctive 4in (10cm) high flowers of a dull red overlaid with olive-green give it an overall curious greenish appearance. *T. linifolia* AGM is a species you could hardly miss, with its cup-shaped, glowing

ABOVE *Tulipa kaufmanniana* 'Showwinner' AGM

scarlet flowers with their violet-black centres. This grows to the same height, flowering in late spring when many of the tulips are past their best. The lady tulip (*T. clusiana*) was first grown in Holland in the very early 1600s. In early spring it produces cherry red outer petals, and inner white petals with a violet base. Also with a long history are *T. praestans* 'Fusilier' AGM, bright red, and 'Unicum', best described as capsicum-red. Both have two to five flowers on 12in (30cm) high stems. *T. acuminata* grows to 18in (45cm), its scarlet and yellow blooms being long and narrow.

Among the first to flower are those from the Kaufmannia group; these brighten up gardens starting in late winter. While the straightforward species, *T. kaufmanniana*, is available it is the named varieties that are best known. Look for: 'Heart's Delight' (ivory white, with the outside of the petals carmine-red edged with pale rose), 'Scarlet Baby' (dazzling scarlet with a yellow base), and 'Showwinner' AGM (white with lovely yellow and red centres). Tulips in this group range in height from 5–8in (12–20cm).

The lily-flowered tulips are unsurpassed for their elegance and charm. Most grow to around 20in (50cm) high, the blooms being easily recognizable by their reflexed petals. Among the best are the deep primrose yellow 'West Point' AGM, the lovely pure white 'White Triumphator' AGM and the eye-catching 'Marilyn', an outstanding white with considerable feathering and flame markings of pink-purple. There are many other tulip categories, but the last one I feel I should mention is the 'single early' range. Look for 'Keizerskroon' AGM (scarlet edged with yellow) and 'Princess Irene' (purple with a lilac flame).

PERENNIALS

ABOVE *Achillea* 'Fanal'

ABOVE *Aethionema* 'Warley Rose' AGM

NAME: *ACHILLEA* (YARROW)

Origin: Temperate regions around the world
USDA Zone: Z6
Description: Yarrow is a pernicious lawn weed, but the decorative perennial types have been bred (predominately in Germany) for flowerheads which bloom for a long period from late spring until early autumn. They can be loose clusters or flat heads comprised of a mass of tiny daisy-like flowers.
Popular species and varieties: *Achillea filipendulina* 'Gold Plate' AGM grows to 4ft (1.2m), and has flat heads of a deep golden yellow. Similar, but shorter at 36in (90cm) is 'Coronation Gold' AGM. 'Fanal' has bright red flowers; 'Apfelblute' (also known as 'Apple Blossom') has flowers of the palest pink.

NAME: *AETHIONEMA*

Origin: Europe, the Mediterranean region and South-west Asia
USDA Zone: Z7
Description: This is a genus of short-lived, evergreen or semi-evergreen perennials and sub-shrubs (and one or two that are distinctly shrub-like). They are grown for their prolific summer flowering. Blooms are wallflower-like (they are related), and generally are shades of pink. They are perfect for the rock garden.
Popular species and varieties: 'Warley Rose' AGM has tiny, linear bluish green leaves, and it comes alive in late spring and summer when the rounded flowerheads of bright pink appear. 'Warley Ruber' is a slightly deeper pink.

NAME: *AGAPANTHUS* (AFRICAN LILY)

Origin: South Africa
USDA Zone: Z7–9
Description: These stunning blue, mop-headed summer perennials range in height from 18–36in (45–90cm). Leaves are dark green, in some cases narrow whilst in others they are

ABOVE *Agapanthus campanulatus* subsp. *patens* AGM

wider and flatter, and plants can be either evergreen or deciduous. These plants should be grown in a sheltered, sunny border, and if you live in a particularly cold district, provide protection in winter by putting down a bark mulch over the root area.

Popular species and varieties: Among the numerous hybrids, a strain known as the Headbourne Hybrids are the best known and most widely available. Flower colours range from deep violet to pale blue. *Agapanthus campanulatus* subsp. *patens* AGM is slightly taller at 4ft (1.2m) and has light blue flowers and greyish leaves.

NAME: *AGAVE AMERICANA* AGM

Origin: North, Central and South America
USDA Zone: Z8–10
Description: I could fill this book with references to the huge cactus and succulent plant groups, as nearly all of them are sun-loving drought-tolerant species. But if you want to form a collection of these for your dry garden, you are better off using a specialized book for your information. I am making an exception of the *Agave* genus, however, as it tends to be seen more in the colder gardens of Northern Europe and North American gardens, and will survive for many years if given winter protection. Agaves are succulent rosette-forming plants with

rigid, fleshy leaves and toothed edges, often tipped with sharp spines. They are excellent for containers and as focal-point architectural plants. Different forms have different ultimate heights, ranging from around 20in–6ft (51cm–2m).

Popular species and varieties: *Agave americana* AGM produces a basal rosette of thick, leathery blue-green leaves. The form 'Variegata' AGM has pale yellow edges to the leaves. 'Mediopicta' AGM has a yellow inner stripe, and 'Mediopicta Alba' AGM has a white inner stripe.

NAME: *AUBRIETA*

Origin: Europe to Central Asia
USDA Zone: Z5–8
Description: This is a hardy evergreen carpeting perennial, producing masses of small, four-petalled flowers in shades of purple, mauve, blue, pink or white during spring. They are indispensable for the rock or scree garden, and are arguably at their best on a low stone wall where they can hang over it. The small leaves are roughly oval.

Popular species and varieties: *Aubrieta* 'Doctor Mules' AGM is deep lilac; 'Red Carpet' is red-purple, and 'Aureovariegata' AGM has pale lavender flowers with green and cream variegated foliage.

ABOVE *Agave americana* 'Variegata' AGM

ABOVE *Aubrieta* 'Doctor Mules' AGM

NAME: *DIANTHUS* (CARNATIONS & PINKS)

Origin: Throughout Europe and Asia
USDA Zone: Z3
Description: A large group of perennials (as well as annuals and biennials), the *Dianthus* is at home in the border, the rockery, containers and even as greenhouse pot plants. All of the perennial forms are evergreen (often with greyish leaves). Carnations are usually larger-flowered, whilst pinks are daintier, and with the serrated edges to the petals (looking as if they have been gone over with a pair of pinking shears, the sort used in dressmaking, which is where the common name of 'pink' arises). Flower colours are variously in shades from white to deep mauve, and every shade of pink and red in between – there are no oranges, yellows or blues.

Popular species and varieties: For the rock garden try *Dianthus alpinus*, with deep pink or reddish flowers, and 'La Barboule' with scented pink flowers. Modern pinks include 'Doris' (pink, double and fragrant) and 'Haytor White' AGM (glistening white). Old-fashioned pinks include 'Mrs Sinkins' (white, double) and 'Dad's Favourite' (red and white, semi-double). *D. amurensis* has an endearing if lax habit, with large flowers in proportion to the plant; my favourite form is 'Siberian Blue', which is more mauve, and with maroon centres to the flowers.

ABOVE *Dianthus amurensis* 'Siberian Blue'

ABOVE *Gazania* Daybreak 'Red Stripe'

NAME: *GAZANIA*

Origin: Africa
USDA Zone: Z9
Description: The *Gazania* is a half-hardy evergreen perennial, much like a *Pelargonium* in growing requirements, and therefore best treated as an annual. A dwarf, spreading plant, it generally has deep green leaves with whitish-grey undersides. Large daisy-like flowers open mainly only in direct sun, although cultivars are being bred to perform better in dull weather. Flowers are produced all summer long. Grow gazanias in summer bedding schemes or in patio containers.

Popular species and varieties: The Chansonette, Daybreak and Mini-Star Series all have flowers that are predominately deep yellow or pale orange, with red and brown-black markings. Plants in the Sundance Series are very free-flowering, but are plainly coloured in shades of yellow, orange and gold.

NAME: *GERANIUM AND PELARGONIUM*

Origin: South Africa
USDA Zone: Z9–10
Description: These plants have been grouped together here. Although they are related botanically, and confusion has always surrounded the naming of them (mainly over the question whether pelargoniums are actually geraniums, even though they commonly go by

the name), they do appear to be entirely different plants. The hardy geraniums, often called cranesbills, are mound-forming plants, often with a lax habit that gets battered during heavy rain. Pelargoniums, on the other hand, are hot weather-loving bedding and pot plants that, though actually tender perennials, are best treated as annuals and discarded at the end of the summer season. Both types warrant inclusion here as they are tolerant of drought conditions.

Popular species and varieties: There are in the region of 400 species of hardy *Geranium*, and at least 200 cultivars of *Pelargonium*, so choosing a mere handful to mention here is an almost impossible task. Of the cranesbills look for *Geranium psilostemon* AGM (magenta), the hybrid 'Anne Folkard' AGM (magenta-purple and darker veining) and *G. sylvaticum* (bright purple with white centres). Of the pelargoniums, I would recommend the Zonal forms (so called because of the darker zones on the upper surfaces of the leaves). Look for the Multibloom, Sensation or Vista series. Flower colours come in bright reds, pinks, white and sometimes mauve.

NAME: *KNIPHOFIA* (RED HOT POKER)

Origin: South Africa
USDA Zone: Z5–7
Description: There is a place for a red hot poker in every garden, regardless of size. Some varieties throw spikes up to 6ft (2m), whilst others – known as the dwarf varieties – are a fraction of the size at just 20in (50cm). These are superb 'architectural' plants in the right setting. It is not hard to see why the common name was applied to the plants, with their flower spikes in shades of red, yellow and orange.

Popular species and varieties: 'Percy's Pride' has sulphur yellow flowers; 'Samuel's Sensation' AGM has scarlet spikes in late summer; 'Candlelight' is a dwarf with pure yellow flowers; and *Kniphofia caulescens* AGM is one of the latest to flower, with yellow, red-tipped flowers that produce colour into mid-autumn.

ABOVE *Geranium sylvaticum*

ABOVE *Pelargonium* 'Century Rose'

ABOVE *Kniphofia caulescens* AGM

ABOVE *Osteospermum* (white hybrid)

NAME: *OSTEOSPERMUM*

Origin: South Africa and the Arabian peninsula
USDA Zone: Z7–9
Description: Mainly evergreen half-hardy to hardy perennials generally grown as annuals, osteospermums are dwarf, low-growing bushy plants producing plentiful daisy-like flowers over a long period from late spring to early autumn. Flowers come in a range of colours. These are best viewed at the front of a border, or in patio containers where the stems can be allowed to drape over the sides.
Popular species and varieties: There are hybrids in white, yellow, purple and pink shades. There are also the 'spoon-flowered' forms where the edges of the central portion of each ray floret are folded together, but the tip of which is fully expanded. The white-flowered 'Whirligig' AGM is the best-known example.

NAME: *ROMNEYA COULTERI* AGM (CALIFORNIA TREE POPPY)

Origin: South-western North America
USDA Zone: Z7
Description: This is an imposing plant with grey foliage and sumptuous, scented flowers that are among the largest in the poppy family. A suckering plant, it has upright stems that, in a good summer, can reach 10ft (3m) in height,

although in practice they are rather less than this. Dramatic, fragrant, white flowers with deep yellow centres, in the usual poppy style of petals like crumpled tissue, are carried either singly, or in threes, at the tips of the shoots throughout summer and autumn. I've often referred to this plant as the 'fried egg plant', and one look at the flowers will show you why.
Popular species and varieties: Only the one species is grown in gardens and there are two different forms available. One is *Romneya coulteri* var. *trichocalyx*, a slightly slimmer form with leaves that are finely divided. The other is the cultivar 'White Cloud' AGM with slightly larger flowers than the straight species.

NAME: *RUDBECKIA* (CONEFLOWER)

Origin: North America
USDA Zone: Z3–7
Description: These hardy perennials are grown for their late-flowering habit. They come into bloom right at the end of summer, just when you are thinking of packing everything away. Suddenly they can give a tired flower border a new lease of life for a month or so. They are daisy-flowered plants, but the daisies are mainly shades of yellow and orange, and some 2in (5cm) or more across.
Popular species and varieties: *Rudbeckia fulgida* var. *sullivantii* 'Goldsturm' AGM is

ABOVE *Romneya coulteri* AGM

ABOVE *Rudbeckia fulgida* var. *sullivantii* 'Goldsturm' AGM

ABOVE Mixed *Sempervivum* spp

arguably the best, with bright golden yellow flowers each with a black central 'cone'. *R. laciniata* 'Goldquelle' AGM has double flowers of chrome yellow, while 'Herbstonne' can reach 7ft (2.1m) with single yellow flowers and greenish centres – perfect for the back of the border.

NAME: *SEMPERVIVUM* (HOUSELEEK)

Origin: Europe, North Africa and Western Asia
USDA Zone: Z4–8
Description: The houseleek offers a solution for those who want to use succulents but are worried about hardiness. From the Latin, the name means 'always alive' – and to prove this, as well as drought, the genus is tolerant of cold weather and poor soil conditions. *Sempervivum* belongs to the succulent Crassulaceae family.

These plants are considered very hardy, although they do not appreciate prolonged wet conditions, doing best in a well-drained, gritty soil. For this reason, they are best suited to being planted in raised beds, rockeries or crevices, and should be put in sunny locations. If planted outdoors in a container, it is recommended that they are brought inside and kept in a cool, dry area during the winter.

Due to the dry conditions of their natural habitat, *Sempervivum* and other family members have developed a mechanism to reduce the amount of water lost through transpiration. 'Crassulacean acid metabolism' enables the plants to keep their stomata closed during the day.

The plants provide a wide range of leaf colours, from green, through pink and brown to dark purple-black. The leaf styles vary also: some are glossy, while others are covered in down; they vary in shape from tall and rounded, to long and thin. The leaves grow in a rosette shape. Flowers are produced at the end of long stalks that appear in the second or third year. The star-shaped blooms are pink, purple, yellow or white. After flowering, the rosette will die off, leaving a space that can be filled by another rosette.

Popular species and varieties: The genus is generally considered to contain more than 40 species and some 1,000 named cultivars but the nomenclature is not clearly defined. Hybridization is common and often plants grown from seed are not true to type, however, growing from offsets ensures uniformity. *Sempervivum* 'Amanda' is a fast-growing cultivar with dark purple-brown, long tapering leaves. 'Apple Blossom' has medium-sized, open rosettes that are apple green with shades of pink in full sun. 'Black Prince' is purplish-black in summer; the leaves are edged with silvery hairs.

CLIMBING PLANTS

NAME: *CLIANTHUS PUNICEUS* AGM (GLORY PEA, or LOBSTER CLAW, or PARROT'S BILL)

Origin: Australia, New Zealand

USDA Zone: Z8

Description: This evergreen tender scrambling shrub must have a sunny wall, and a well drained soil, and it should be given some winter protection (such as horticultural fleece draped over it when the weather is icy cold). It grows to about 13ft (4m). The flowers are claw-like, and of a brilliant red, gracefully hanging off the plant in drooping clusters during late spring and into early summer.

Popular species and varieties: Normally just the species is seen, but there is a good white form, *C. puniceus* 'Albus' AGM, and a pink form, 'Roseus'.

NAME: *HEDERA* (IVY)

Origin: Europe, Asia, North Africa

USDA Zone: Z5–8

Description: The ivy, certainly in most western countries, must rank as one of the commonest of climbers. It can tolerate quite dense shade, where no other climber would survive. The often-made comment that these plants are dull actually annoys me. As a youngster I assisted in putting together a collection of more than 400 ivies for the world-famous Chelsea Flower Show, and was amazed then at the wealth of variety and colour available – and it still surprises me today. These climbers have clinging aerial roots, enabling them to adhere to whatever it is they are climbing, without the need for tying in.

ABOVE *Clianthus puniceus* AGM

ABOVE *Hedera helix* 'Oro di Bogliasco'

ABOVE *Jasminum nudiflorum* AGM

Popular species and varieties: The common ivy, *Hedera helix*, has relatively small leaves. The larger-leaved forms are generally the more tender *Hedera colchica* and *H. canariensis*. Among these larger types there are none better than 'Sulphur Heart' AGM (pale green leaves with paler green and yellow blotches) and 'Dentata Variegata' AGM (leaves of mid-green and deep cream). *H. canariensis* 'Gloire de Marengo' AGM (dark green leaves with silver-grey surround and white margins) is also wonderful. Among the smaller leaf types, one of the best is 'Oro di Bogliasco' (green leaves with a golden central blotch); also excellent is 'Buttercup' (golden yellow, especially when the leaves are young).

NAME: *JASMINUM NUDIFLORUM* AGM (WINTER JASMINE)

Origin: Northern China
USDA Zone: Z6
Description: This is not so much a true climber, it is more of a scrambling shrub that likes to grow along walls and up trelliswork panels. It bears scentless trifoliate (three-lobed) flowers of bright yellow on its bare green stems in winter and early spring. It is very hardy, and flowers well even in shady places.

Popular species and varieties: Mainly the straight species is grown; although there are a couple of cultivars that vary slightly, they are not significantly different. The summer-flowering jasmines are also popular but in my experience these have not tended to be so drought-tolerant.

143

ABOVE *Passiflora caerulea* AGM

NAME: *PASSIFLORA* (PASSIONFLOWER)

Origin: Brazil, Argentina, United States

USDA Zone: Z7

Description: There are several kinds of passionflower, and they all need watering well for the first year or so until they are established, after which they are reasonably drought-tolerant. If you are growing the edible kinds for their fruits, you will need to irrigate them more frequently in dry summers.

Popular species and varieties: *Passiflora caerulea* AGM is probably the best-known form, with its distinctive blue fringe to the rather complex flower arrangement. The dark green lobed leaves are pleasant enough, but passionflowers are often shy to bloom, even in a sheltered spot. 'Constance Elliott' is ivory white with yellow anthers. The maypop (*P. incarnata*) is the hardiest species, with somewhat smaller flowers yet still showy; it is actually a perennial climber, dying to the ground in winter but rapidly growing the following year to reach 20ft (6m) or so by late summer.

NAME: *PARTHENOCISSUS* (VIRGINIA CREEPER, BOSTON IVY)

Origin: China, Japan, Eastern US to Mexico

USDA Zone: Z3–7

Description: The common name of Virginia creeper seems to be used for both *Parthenocissus tricuspidata* and *P. quinquefolia*, although the former should really be called the Boston ivy. Its hand-like leaves are roughly similar to those of ivy, whereas the creeper's leaves are five-lobed and hence more delicate in appearance. These creeping plants, that will more or less completely cover a wall so that you cannot see the brickwork, make such a fabulous spectacle in autumn, when the leaves turn red, that it can almost take your breath away.

Popular species and varieties: *Parthenocissus tricuspidata* 'Veitchii' is a superb creeper with rather small, three-lobed reddish-purple leaves; *P. quinquefolia* AGM has leaves of five lobes, with similar colouring but is less dense in habit; *P. henryana* AGM produces very dramatic, large bronze-green leaves.

ABOVE *Parthenocissus tricuspidata* AGM

NAME: *WISTERIA*

Origin: China, Japan, Eastern US
USDA Zone: Z4–8
Description: Wisterias are drought-tolerant once they are established in the ground – before this you will need to check them for moisture during dry periods. They are springtime wonders, being so vigorous that they often burst forth in full flower before their leaves have opened. Belonging to the pea family, they produce long trusses of flowers in shades of blue, purple and white. Masses of leaves are produced by mid-summer, and these turn to golden yellow in autumn, often giving the *Wisteria* a second season of interest. They can perform reasonably well in part shade, but in full sun they really come alive.

Popular species and varieties: The Japanese wisteria (*W. floribunda*) can produce stems as long as 28ft (9m) or so. There is a white form, 'Alba'; the form 'Royal Purple' has double, deep purple flowers. The Chinese wisteria (*W. sinensis* AGM) has very fragrant flowers of pale purple, but even better as a plant, although not purple, is the form 'Alba' AGM, with pure white flowers. Both forms of *W. sinensis* make huge plants extending to 100ft (30m) if allowed.

ABOVE *Wisteria sinensis* AGM

TREES AND SHRUBS

ABOVE *Abelia grandiflora* 'Frances Mason'

NAME: *ABELIA*

Origin: China, Japan and the warmer parts of the Himalayas, Mexico

Type: Deciduous, semi-evergreen and evergreen shrubs

USDA Zone: Z5–8

Description: The blooms of *Abelia* are tubular to bell-shaped in a fusion of petals. Their colour can range from white through to red. Individually the flowers are somewhat small, but they come in such profusion, and over a long period in summer and the first half of autumn.

Popular species and varieties: *Abelia grandiflora* 'Francis Mason' has white flowers, and the leaves are flushed orange when young. *A. schumannii* flowers from early summer through to mid-autumn, with bright pink flowers. The hybrid *A.* 'Edward Goucher' has lavender-pink flowers with glossy, semi-evergreen foliage. *A.* 'Gold Spot' is white, and the foliage is variegated with yellow.

NAME: *BRACHYGLOTTIS* (NEW ZEALAND SENECIO)

Origin: New Zealand, Tasmania

Type: Evergreen shrubs

USDA Zone: Z8

Description: The evergreen *Brachyglottis* is a particularly good shrub for exposed, coastal places, as it tolerates salt spray, but that does not mean it should be grown just in such places. It produces a mass of yellow dandelion-like flowers throughout summer. However, it is the grey, felt-leaved foliage that is considered by many to be the most endearing feature. These shrubs used to be called, and are still widely referred to as, *Senecio*. However, the true *Senecio* genus also includes such weeds as ragwort and groundsel, so in the late 1980s horticultural authorities agreed to give the plant its own genus – *Brachyglottis*.

Popular species and varieties: *Brachyglottis* 'Sunshine' AGM is the best form by far with its bright yellow flowers and silvery-grey leaves, particularly when they are young. *B. monroi* AGM has a slightly denser habit, and its leaves have wavy edges.

NAME: *CARYOPTERIS* (BLUEBEARD)

Origin: Eastern Asia

Type: Deciduous shrubs

USDA Zone: Z6–8

Description: You are most likely to see *Caryopteris x clandonensis*, a hybrid between *C. incana* from Japan and *C. mongolica* from Mongolia. It has leaves of grey-green, and the bright blue flowers are carried in late summer and early autumn. It is a good shrub for mixed borders, where it should be located towards the front so it can be appreciated close-up.

Popular species and varieties: *Caryopteris x clandonensis* 'Arthur Simmonds' AGM is a prolific flowerer, and very reliable. 'Worcester

ABOVE *Brachyglottis* 'Sunshine' AGM

ABOVE *Caryopteris* 'Worcester Gold' AGM

Gold' AGM is a rather more compact version and has mid-blue with yellow-green foliage flowers of a slightly darker blue. Little breeding work has taken place with *Caryopteris* generally, but this is changing. Over the next decade a number of cultivars are set to be launched, so this is a genus to watch.

NAME: *CEANOTHUS* (CALIFORNIAN LILAC)

Origin: North America, particularly California
Type: Evergreen and deciduous shrubs
USDA Zone: Z4–8
Description: These shrubs are very different from the common lilac (*Syringa*). The evergreen varieties should be grown under the protection of a sheltered, warm wall; they do not appear to be very successful where they may be subjected to cold winds. The deciduous forms are generally tougher. Most flower from mid- to late spring, the blooms being varying shades of blue. Some of the later-flowering forms are pink.
Popular species and varieties: The Monterey ceanothus (*Ceanothus cuneatus* var. *rigidus*) has deep lavender-coloured flowers, and reaches 4ft (1.2m). C. 'Blue Mound' AGM produces dense clusters of mid-blue flowers; 'Blue

Cushion' is deep blue with a neat, spreading habit, and 'Cynthia Postan' is deep blue with a bushy form. Among the deciduous forms is 'Gloire de Versailles' AGM with large heads of pale blue flowers in mid-summer.

ABOVE *Ceanothus cuneatus* var. *rigidus*

ABOVE *Cistus* x *purpureus* **AGM**

ABOVE *Cotinus coggygria* 'Royal Purple' AGM

NAME: *CISTUS* (ROCK ROSE, or SUN ROSE)

Origin: Mediterranean region
Type: Evergreen shrubs
USDA Zone: Z7–8
Description: Only plant this shrub if you have a sunny spot – try it anywhere else and it will fail. It copes exceedingly well with a fairly impoverished and dry soil. The flowers last for just a day – actually, sometimes just a morning, with the petals all but gone by mid-afternoon. However, the blooms come in such profusion that you hardly notice this. White is the principal flower colour, followed by pink, but most forms have petals marked with various blotches.
Popular species and varieties: *Cistus x purpureus* AGM features masses of large, rich pink flowers with maroon blotches on neat 4ft (1.2m) high bushes. *C. x dansereaui* has saucer-shaped blooms of pure white, each with a central deep red blotch. *C. albidus* has lovely light pink flowers from late spring to mid-summer; however, this is not a long-lived plant, and a severe winter may cause its demise.

NAME: *COTINUS* (SMOKE TREE)

Origin: North America, Southern Europe, China and the Himalayas
Type: Deciduous shrubs and trees
USDA Zone: Z5
Description: This shrub produces wispy flowers that smother it from early summer onwards – a smoky sort of appearance, hence the common name. Most forms have purple foliage, and in these the flower stalks have a purplish tinge. In the green form the stalks start a shade of fawn and end as smoky grey. Most grow to just 6ft (2m) or so, occasionally bigger.
Popular species and varieties: *Cotinus coggygria* AGM has rounded, mid-green leaves that take on fine autumn colour. 'Royal Purple' AGM has deep wine-red foliage, become red in autumn. 'Flame' AGM produces clusters of pink flowers and, not surprisingly, turns to a flame-red in autumn.

NAME: *CYTISUS* (BROOM)

Origin: North Africa, Western Asia, Europe
Type: Deciduous and evergreen shrubs
USDA Zone: Z5–9
Description: The brooms are very floriferous members of the pea and bean family. Few people would fail to notice one in full flower, covered with masses of blooms in yellow, cream, orange and red tones. You can choose from prostrate shrubs to bushes of 12ft (4m) or more in height. They are excellent for the mixed border, and very successful on hot, dry banks. The lower-growing forms develop into mounds, and these can look particularly good when allowed to flop over a low wall. The leaves of brooms (with the exception of *Cytisus battandieri*) are transient, and most of the plant's photosynthesis takes place within the stems and stalks. These shrubs are fast-growing but, unfortunately, not long-lived.

Popular species and varieties: *Cytisus* 'Burkwoodii' AGM flowers in late spring to early summer, with blooms of cerise, the wings of which are deep crimson edged with yellow. There are a number of new hybrids that are worth growing, including 'La Coquette' (a mixture of rose-red, orange-red and yellow shades) and 'Killiney Salmon' (salmon pink). A completely different habit is to be had with my favourite *Cytisus* of all, the 12ft (4m) high *C. battandieri* AGM, known as the pineapple broom, because the golden yellow flowers do actually smell similar, and are relatively pineapple-shaped.

NAME: *GENISTA* (BROOM)

Origin: Europe, Middle East
Type: Deciduous, almost leafless shrubs
USDA Zone: Z5–9
Description: Closely related to *Cytisus*, forms of *Genista* are particularly noted for their free-flowering nature. Many are ideal for ground cover, or for dry banks or low walls. All produce flowers in shades of yellow or cream.

ABOVE *Cytisus* 'La Coquette'

ABOVE *Genista tinctoria* 'Flore Pleno' AGM

Popular species and varieties: Some genistas have spines, but of the common garden forms only *Genista hispanica*, appropriately referred to as Spanish gorse, is really spiny. It grows to 2ft (60cm) and covers itself with bright yellow flowers in late spring and early summer. *G. lydia* AGM is perfect for the rock garden, or tumbling over a low wall. Its foliage, such as it is, disappears under a profusion or bright yellow flowers. *G. tinctoria* 'Flore Pleno' AGM has double flowers of bright golden yellow.

NAME: *HEBE*

Origin: New Zealand, Australia, South America
Type: Evergreen shrubs
USDA Zone: Z6–9
Description: *Hebe* flowers usually come in bottlebrush-like clusters at the ends of the shoots, each bloom comprising four petals joined at the base. Most natural or wild forms of *Hebe* have white flowers, but over the years shades of pink, blue, purple and red have been bred. The leaves come in two main forms: they are either the large-leaved types such as you get with the cultivars 'Autumn Glory' and 'Caledonia' AGM, and then there are the so-called 'whipcord' types, where the leaves are tight to the stems and scale-like, rather like a *Cupressus* (cypress) in appearance. Hebes are fairly short-lived shrubs, and they vary considerably in their hardiness.
Popular species and varieties: Some of the best of the large-leaved types for displaying their charms in a dry garden include: *Hebe* 'Caledonia' AGM, violet blooms, each with a white eye; 'Baby Marie', pale lilac flowers on brown stems, growing to just 8in (20cm) in height;

'Autumn Glory', purple flowers and large dark green leaves with a reddish margin, up to 3ft (90cm) high; 'Great Orme' AGM, bright pink flowers; 'Margret' AGM, rich blue flowers and bright green leaves. Of the 'whipcord' types I would look for *H. ochracea* 'James Stirling' AGM, golden foliage and white flowers; and *H. armstrongii*, olive-green foliage and white flowers. All reach a height of around 18in (45cm).

NAME: *HELIANTHEMUM* (SUN ROSE, or ROCK ROSE)

Origin: American Continent, Mediterranean region, North Africa, Asia
Type: Evergreen shrubs and sub-shrubs
USDA Zone: Z7
Description: These plants are easy to grow, thriving in relatively poor conditions; they are most suited to rock gardens, or pockets on walls, or the front of borders. They are available in either single or double flower forms, and the main colours are white, crimson, pink, flamed-red, copper-orange and yellow. Individual blooms last for just a day, but there are usually

ABOVE *Hebe* 'Baby Marie'

ABOVE *Helianthemum* 'Rhodanthe Carneum' AGM

ABOVE *Lavandula* 'Helmsdale'

so many blooms covering the plants from late spring to mid-summer that this does not matter.

Popular species and varieties: Both the rich golden yellow 'Henfield Brilliant' AGM, and the paler yellow 'Wisley Primrose' AGM are personal favourites. But I also adore 'Rhodanthe Carneum' AGM with rose pink petals and a central boss of golden stamens. There are at least 13 excellent cultivars with the prefix 'Ben'. Some of the best include 'Ben Fahda' (bright yellow and leaves of grey-green); 'Ben Macdhui' (orange), 'Ben Nevis' (orange-yellow) and 'Ben Heckla' (copper-orange).

NAME: *LAVANDULA* (LAVENDER)

Origin: Mediterranean region, North Africa, Western Asia, Arabia, India
Type: Evergreen shrubs
USDA Zone: Z5–9

Description: Lavender is among the best known of all garden shrubs, and epitomizes dry soil and a sun-drenched climate. It is valued particularly for its aromatic foliage and flowers. The silver leaves ensure that plants are decorative even when they are not in flower. The name 'lavender' comes from the water that is made from the oil; *lavo* being latin for 'wash'.

Popular species and varieties: *Lavandula angustifolia* is the old English lavender with pale blue flowers on long stems. A white form ('Alba') is available. Of the cultivars, 'Hidcote' AGM (violet flowers), 'Hidcote Pink' (with pink flowers) and 'Nana Alba' (white flowers on a dwarf form) are to my mind superior. The French lavender (*L. stoechas* AGM) has become very popular in recent years. It has dark purple flowers borne in dense, congested heads topped by distinctive terminal bracts. 'Helmsdale' flowers freely with even deeper blooms.

151

ABOVE *Phlomis fruticosa* AGM

ABOVE *Rosmarinus officinalis* 'Miss Jessop's Upright' AGM

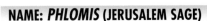

NAME: *PHLOMIS* (JERUSALEM SAGE)

Origin: Mediterranean region to Central Asia and China
Type: Evergreen shrubs
USDA Zone: Z7–9
Description: Grown for its combination of attractive flowers and foliage, this is an exotic-looking shrub with felted leaves and stems. The flowers are clustered into whorls along the upright stems; individually the flowers are tubular with a hooded upper lip, resembling the blooms of the dead nettle. It is a member of the Labiatae plant family, which has lavender, sage and *Euonymus* as kin.
Popular species and varieties: *Phlomis fruticosa* AGM has bright golden yellow flowers. It makes a shrub about 4ft (1.2m) high, or slightly less. *P. chrysophylla* AGM is similar but the leaves have a golden-green tinge. The pink or pale lilac flowered *P. italica* is much smaller, rarely exceeding 12in (30cm) in height.

NAME: *ROSMARINUS* (ROSEMARY)

Origin: Southern Europe, North Africa
Type: Evergreen shrubs
USDA Zone: Z6–8
Description: Rosemary, classed as a 'woody herb', is grown for its aromatic foliage, with sprigs used for flavouring and scenting various meat and fish dishes. They also make fine and decorative garden plants. Some shelter from prevailing winds is desirable, along with a sunny location and a dryish soil.
Popular species and varieties: *Rosmarinus officinalis* is the usual species grown. It reaches around 5ft (1.5m) in height, and has narrow grey-green leaves and clusters of small, pale blue flowers in spring and early summer. More upright, or fastigiated in habit is 'Miss Jessop's Upright' AGM. The prostrate form 'McConnell's Blue' AGM, can be used on a rockery, and is good grown in a patio container where it can tumble over the sides.

ABOVE *Santolina chamaecyparissus*

NAME: *SANTOLINA* (COTTON LAVENDER)

Origin: Mediterranean region
Type: Evergreen shrubs
USDA Zone: Z7
Description: Even when not in flower, the tight, silver-grey, very finely divided leaves make santolinas worth growing. The flowers are in small, button-like heads carried above the foliage on long stalks in mid- to late summer. These make small, evergreen shrubs, and can be trimmed into mini-hedges. As with lavender and rosemary, these plants have an overriding need for full sun and a well-drained to dry soil.
Popular species and varieties: The form that is most widely seen in gardens is *Santolina chamaecyparissus* AGM, with silver cypress-like foliage and bright yellow flowers. *S. pinnata* subsp. *neapolitana* AGM has lemon-yellow flowers, whilst a cultivar of it – 'Sulphurea' – has flowers of a warmer yellow.

NAME: *VINCA* (PERIWINKLE)

Origin: Northern Asia, Europe
Type: Low, ground-covering shrub
USDA Zone: Z4–9
Description: In the landscape, vincas are most effective when trailing over and covering a bank, and they will readily colonize dry, shady places under trees. The common name of periwinkle comes from the Middle English *per wynke*, referring to wreath making, for the long, flexible stems of *Vinca* are suitable for winding around, and binding, curved frames. The flowers are nearly always shades of blue but a few are white.
Popular species and varieties: *V. major* is the large or greater periwinkle. It's a vigorous, shrubby, carpeting or trailing shrub that provides excellent dense cover except on exposed sites or on poorly drained soils. Its star-shaped flowers are blue or white and appear in spring. *V. major* 'Variegata' has leaves with pale green blotches and margins of cream-yellow; the flowers are in shades of violet. One of its parents is *V. major* var. *oxyloba*, which is very vigorous, forming a dense rampant cover. *V. minor* is the dwarf or lesser periwinkle. It is a smaller-leaved species, but nevertheless offers very effective ground cover in similar conditions.

ABOVE *Vinca major*

Glossary

Acid
With a pH value below 7; acid soil is deficient in lime and basic minerals.

Alkaline
With a pH value above 7.

Annual
Plant grown from seed that germinates, flowers, sets seed and dies in one growing year.

Bare-root
Plants sold with their roots bare of soil (ie. not in a pot or container).

Biennial
A plant that grows from seed and completes its life cycle within two years.

Cultivar
A cultivated plant clearly distinguished by one or more characteristics and which retains these characteristics when propagated; a contraction of 'cultivated variety', and often abbreviated to 'cv.' in plant naming.

Deciduous
Plant that loses its leaves at the end of every growing year, and which renews them at the start of the next.

Double
Referred to in flower terms as a bloom with several layers of petals; usually there would be a minimum of 20 petals. 'Very double' flowers have more than 40 petals.

Genus (pl. Genera)
A category in plant naming, comprising a group of related species.

Heeling in
Laying plants in the soil, with the roots covered, as a temporary measure until full planting can take place.

Humus
Organic matter that has decomposed in the soil and has been broken down by bacteria, resulting in a black, crumbly substance from which plants can easily extract nutrients.

Hybrid
The offspring of genetically different parents, usually produced in cultivation, but occasionally arising in the wild.

Mulch
Layer of material applied to the soil surface, to conserve moisture, improve its structure, protect roots from frost, and suppress weeds.

Perennial
Plant that lives for at least three years.

Photosynthesis
The process of food manufacture in plants, whereby chlorophyll in leaves traps the sun's energy, combines it with carbon dioxide in the air and hydrogen in water and creates carbohydrates.

pH scale
A scale measured from 1–14 that indicates the alkalinity or acidity of soil. pH 7 is neutral; pH 1–7 is acid, pH 7–14 is alkaline.

Ray floret
The 'petals' of the flowers of some members of the daisy family.

Rootstock
A plant used to provide the root system for a grafted plant.

Scorch
Leaves turning brown and dry, mainly as a result of bright sunlight and hot weather (also cold winds and chemical spray damage).

Sideshoot
A stem that arises from the side of a main shoot or stem.

Single
In flower terms, a single layer of petals opening out into a fairly flat shape, comprising no more than five petals.

Species
A category in plant naming, the rank below genus, containing related, individual plants.

Stomata
Microspopic pores on the undersides of leaves. They control the water content of the plant by opening, to allow transpiration, and closing to prevent it.

Sub-shrub
A plant that produces some woody mature growth, but the soft growth of which will die down in winter.

Sucker
Generally a shoot that arises from below ground, emanating from a plant's roots, but also refers to any shoot on a grafted plant that originates from below the graft union.

Transpiration
Part of the natural process of photosynthesis whereby plants lose water through their leaves into the atmosphere. Should the rate of transpiration exceed the rate of water intake via the roots, the plant will dehydrate and then start to wilt.

Variety
Botanically, a naturally occurring variant of a wild species. It is usually shorted to 'var.' in plant naming.

Xeriscape
A type of landscaping which makes use of items of hard landscaping such as rocks, cobbles, gravel, slate and even wood, to form an almost maintenance-free design. It developed in the hot, dry south-western United States, out of a need to save water.

About the author

Graham Clarke lives in Dorset, on England's south coast, with his wife and two daughters. Here the air is clear, with a mild climate that is far drier than most other parts of the UK.

Graham was born into gardening – literally. His father was in charge of the world-famous Regent's Park in London and, at the time of Graham's birth, the family lived in a lodge within the gardens. During his formative years Graham was surrounded by quality horticulture, so it was little surprise when he chose this as his career. He went to study with England's Royal Horticultural Society at Wisley Gardens, and after that worked as a gardener at Buckingham Palace in London. This very private garden is seen by Her Majesty the Queen on most of the days she is in residence.

For more than 25 years Graham has been a gardening writer and journalist. He has written eight books, and countless articles for most of the major UK gardening magazines. At various times he was editor of *Amateur Gardening* (the UK's leading weekly magazine for amateurs) and *Horticulture Week* (the UK's leading weekly magazine for professionals).

Index

Illustrations of plants are indicated by page numbers in **bold**

GMC Publications Ltd, 166 High Street, Lewes, East Sussex BN7 1XU, United Kingdom
Tel: 01273 488005 Fax: 01273 402866
www.gmcbooks.com
Contact us for a complete catalogue, or visit our website.